The Impossible
Science

Volume 181 Sage Library of Social Research

RECENT VOLUMES IN . . .
SAGE LIBRARY OF SOCIAL RESEARCH

The Impossible Science

Science

An Institutional
Analysis of
American Sociology

Stephen Park Turner
Jonathan H. Turner

Sage Library of Social Research 181

SAGE PUBLICATIONS
The International Professional Publishers
Newbury Park   London   New Delhi

For information address:

SAGE Publications, Inc.
2111 West Hillcrest Drive
Newbury Park, California 91320

SAGE Publications Ltd.
28 Banner Street
London EC1Y 8QE
England

SAGE Publications India Pvt. Ltd.
M-32 Market
Greater Kailash I
New Delhi 110 048 India

Printed in the United States of America

Library of Congress Cataloging-in-Publication Data

Turner, Stephen P., 1951 -
  The impossible science: an institutional analysis of American sociology / Stephen Park Turner, Jonathan H. Turner.
    p. cm. — (Sage library of social research: v. 181)
  Includes bibliographical references and index.
  ISBN 0-8039-3838-1.— ISBN 0-8039-3839-X (pbk.)
  1. Sociology— United States —History.— I. Turner, Jonathan H.
II. Title. III. Series
HM22.U5T87   1990
301′.0973—dc20   90-8553
                                                              CIP

FIRST PRINTING, 1990

Sage Production Editor: Astrid Virding

Contents

Preface

The first significant American sociologists—Lester Frank Ward, Franklin Giddings, Albion Small, and even William Graham Sumner—were committed to a scientific approach. Auguste Comte and Herbert Spencer were frequently quoted and viewed as the exemplars of how to undertake the scientific analysis of society. Yet this early optimism declined in the decades of this century, culminating in the present state of division between those who are committed to sociology as a science and those who remain skeptical and critical of such pretensions.

Much of the debate over the prospects for sociology as a science has been conducted at a philosophical level, and, as such, it has often consisted of shrill pronouncements by scholars who simply talk past one another. More recently, in the aftermath of Thomas Kuhn's analysis of "scientific revolutions," philosophical discourse has been supplemented by the analysis of scientific organizations and the ways in which they produce knowledge. These organizational approaches are often used to mount philosophical criticisms about the "objectivity" of all science, and especially the social sciences, but they are also used to analyze science as an organized activity.

The most useful outcome of these organizational approaches is the view that science is a social process—a line of emphasis that shifts debate away from purely philosophical discourse toward empirical investigation of scientists. Of course, historical and present-day descriptions of how groups of scientists go about their trade are frequently used to debunk and criticize notions of a "logic of discovery" in science. Yet, they nonetheless provide useful data. At the same time, more theoretical models have also been produced in an effort to understand the data on various historical and contemporary cases.

We mention these trends in order to place into context the title of this book, *The Impossible Science*. At a philosophical level, the authors hold very different opinions about the feasibility of a scientific sociology—J. H. Turner (1985) believing that it is, in principle, possible to produce sociological knowledge like that in the natural sciences, and S. P. Turner (1990a) arguing that the cognitive successes of sociology should be interpreted differently. But whatever our philosophical disagreements, we agree that the organization of sociology as a whole hinders its development as a science. For J. H. Turner, this situation represents a great tragedy, whereas for S. P. Turner such histrionics seem unwarranted. In any case, our sense that the organization of sociology is central to understanding why sociology has not developed as a science led us to examine the institutional structure of American sociology as it has developed over the last 100 years. As we proceeded, it became increasingly evident that the nature of the resource base for conducting sociological activity was central to understanding both the emergence and subsequent development of American sociology. We did not begin with this notion; rather, it simply became an inescapable conclusion as we explored the institutionalization of sociology in America from the 1890s to the present.

Many others have, of course, described the history of sociology, and we will make reference to their works. But none has adopted the theme of this book: The structure of sociology as an academic discipline and the production of ideas is intimately connected to the nature and level of resources that have been available to sociologists. Of course, there is no one-to-one correspondence between the organization of a discipline and the nature of its knowledge, on the one side, and the types and amount of resources available to it, on the other. Ideas do reveal internal logics which are forces in their own right. Startling break-throughs can take a discipline in a certain direction. Chance events may have a crucial effect on what course a discipline pursues. And, internal politics and conflicts often dictate the organization of a profession. Yet there is always a resource base for even these kinds of processes. Ideas are produced by people in organizations who require money, time, intellectual capital, colleagues, students, libraries, physical facilities, and other re-sources. New discoveries often require equipment, organization, and money to be generated as well as accepted. Chance events are often rather highly circumscribed by the organizational, fi-nancial, and cultural forces that "load the dice" for certain kinds of intellectual production. And, the politics and conflicts of a discipline are frequently over who is to control what resources.

The present nature of a discipline such as sociology is thus a reflection of past effects of the resources available to, and used by, cohorts of individuals who sought to create and then sustain an intellectual enterprise. To understand American sociology, we believe, requires a historical perspective on how those who call themselves sociologists mobilized varying types of resources. For the theories, methods, and substance that have emerged in Amer-ican sociology have been influenced by the shifting profile of resources available to, and used by, sociologists as they sought to forge a discipline within the American academic system. The end result was to produce a discipline the very organization of which precludes its integration in terms of science. Sociology has thus become "the impossible science."

Acknowledgments

The support of the Academic Senate, University of California at Riverside, is acknowledged, with appreciation and thanks for its support of J. H. Turner's work over the years. The unpaid assistance of David Waller, a Ph.D. candidate at the University of California, Riverside, was invaluable in tracking down books, references, and data sources. The members of Stephen Turner's seminar, The History of Quantification in Sociology, at Boston University in 1987 are also gratefully acknowledged.

We are grateful for the assistance of the archivists at the following universities: Harvard, Columbia, Chicago, Duke, and North Carolina; as well as the archivists at the Columbia Oral History Office. Material from the Bernard papers is quoted by permission of Jessie Bernard and the Department of Special Collections, the University of Chicago Library. Quotations from the Samuel A. Stouffer papers are quoted by permission of the Harvard University Archives and Ann S. Bisconti. Quotations from and citations to the Reminiscences of Helen Lynd, Robert MacIver, and Frederick Keppel in the Oral History Collection of Columbia University are by permission of the Oral History Research Office of Columbia University.

ONE

The Academicization of Reform: American Sociology Before World War I

In 1880, the editor of *The Popular Science Monthly* was moved to proclaim:

> No intelligent man will deny that social order is based upon natural laws, and exemplifies cause and effect. Social phenomena may be analyzed and classified, and reduced to general expressions or principles, like other phenomena of Nature. . . . It is no longer a question that these social laws shall be worked out as an independent body of science. (Editor, 1880)

These bold comments come from an editorial on the dispute between William Graham Sumner and the president of Yale over the teaching of sociology. Seemingly, many at Yale had objected to the use of Herbert Spencer's methodological textbook, *The Study of Sociology* (1873), and the introduction of "scientific" methods into a realm that traditionally had been dominated by other fields, particularly religion and moral philosophy. The legitimizing umbrella of "science" was not to go unchallenged in 1880, however, and as we will come to see, over a hundred years later, the scientific pretensions of sociology are still controversial. What seemed so possible to the editor of *The Popular Science*

Monthly and to many early sociologists was, in fact, to become increasingly problematic.

SOCIOLOGY AS REFORM, RELIGION, AND SCIENCE

Even at the time that the editor of *The Popular Science Monthly* made his confident pronouncement, there was still considerable uncertainty about what sociology was, or could be. For by 1880 the term *sociology* had numerous connotations in the United States. In addition to its association with the scientism of Auguste Comte and Herbert Spencer, the label "sociology" embraced such activities as philanthropic and reform efforts to help the "dependent classes," public edification on the need for social reform, attempts at making the church more effective in the social arena, arguments bolstering the intellectual authority of the cooperative movement, and programs for collecting statistics on the laboring classes. Each of these associations was embodied in some form of work, ranging from reformist activity and government research to college teaching and literary writings. All of these activities required a resource base. For example, reform organizations had membership dues and sold subscriptions to their publications; government statistical work was financed out of taxation; church activities were financed by members' contributions. For many of the persons involved, these activities were avocations, with ministerial work or journalism being their primary source of income. The origins of the first generation of academic sociologists were thus diverse, with the line between professional sociology and other activities unclear.

One or two courses with such titles as "The Philosophy of Social Relations" had been offered before the American Civil War (1860-1865) (Morgan, 1982, p. 27). In the first two decades after the war, several more were given, though their content and character were not regularized. One common theme, however, was the problem of social reform. The social reform movements of the day thus provided the subject matter and ideological *problemata* to which the academic courses were oriented. And the movement and literature of reformism far outstripped academic forms of sociology. It should not be surprising, therefore, that among the first dozen or so presidents of the American Sociological Society, most were persons with a background in reform movements of one kind or another. In fact, none of the four "founders" of American sociology—Lester Ward, William Graham Sumner, Franklin H. Giddings, and Albion Small—had originally prepared for an academic career. Sumner and Small were theologically trained; Giddings was a journalist; and Ward a government paleobotanist.

Each of these founders developed his distinctive views in an intellectual world formed largely by the set of interrelated reform movements that developed after the Civil War[1] and, in a sense, were a continuation of the moral impulses of abolitionists in the pre-Civil War period. These movements provided opportunities to write, edit, lecture, engage in practical politics and philanthropy, and, on occasion, perform empirical research. The organizations that housed these movements have few parallels today because many of their activities have become a part of the government.

Most of the these organizations were motivated by the abhorrence of some sort of activity or practice, such as vice, divorce, drunkenness, improper entertainment for the young, and the like. What was novel in the immediate aftermath of the Civil War was the sense that these evils could be overcome through public crusades of edification, legislation, and regulation. The newly visible problems associated with urbanization and industrialization, notably the problem of unemployment in the cities resulting from war demobilization, provided a new arena for the reformist temper. In most of the areas that reformers entered, however, the intellectual content of the "cause" was not very imposing: the evils and their solutions were thought to be obvious, and it was a Christian obligation to act against them.[2] These practical aims pervaded the reading and writing of what was called "social science" at the time, and when reformers spoke of "the need for social science," they meant the need to educate the population and change opinion. The content of "social science" was not considered problematic; it was simply the conclusions that would be reached by "right-thinking persons" who reflected on the issues of corrections, charities, and the labor problem. Not surprisingly, the airing of opinions on these subjects led to a certain degree of disagreement, but for the most part it was disagreement between persons engaged in a common practical task. But there were some systematic sources of tension as well. In particular, there were individuals whose ties to religion were weak, and hence, problems for them were not so easily viewed as conflicts between good and evil. As a result, questions of labor, immigration, and monetary policy gave rise to more concerted intellectual effort than did such topics as the suppression of vice. Here, the reform thinkers could meet a need for guidance beyond the vague demands of the Bible and the Protestant conscience that had sufficed for the abolitionists in the pre-Civil War era (1830-1860). But the view of sociology as "science" was to create new intellectual tensions, since much science was seen to be blasphemous in 19th-century America.

These tensions among religion, education, and science were the topics of the first books on sociology and social science in the period after the Civil War. Indeed, a lively "higher journalism" on such reform questions as divorce arose during the period. Some of this journalism was specifically identified as "sociological," and some of the persons who were to become "sociologists" were first interested in the subject matter through reading such general intellectual journals as the *North American Review*.

The activities of the protosociologists in this period clearly served the purposes of others, particularly reformers. The academicization of sociology did not change sociology's dependence on these clients and patrons, however. For the goals of the reformers were essential to early sociology's ability to support itself, recruit students, and command a public audience. These patronage relationships changed over time, and the links became less direct, but the fundamental dependence of American sociology on its service to reform did not disappear. The research activities of the protosociologists, several of whom were to become academic sociologists, exhibit this dependence most directly because their work required extensive funding and, at the same time, was politically visible and controversial.

THE ORIGINS OF EMPIRICAL RESEARCH IN AMERICAN SOCIOLOGY

The American tradition of systematic social survey emerged as a consequence of the economic dislocations during the decade after the Civil War. The problems of "labor" became an important part of popular consciousness and, in the eastern states especially, an element in state politics. For example, the founding of the Massachusetts Bureau of Statistics of Labor in 1869 involved an effort to sort out the claims about the number of unemployed and to determine if returning Civil War veterans were taking the jobs of the already employed or were themselves unemployed.

The initial resource base of the "labor statistics" movement was explicitly political: it was a concession to the interests of the working classes, although a concession which, at the time, was perceived to be insufficient. The "objectivity" of the results was not especially problematic since, like testimony in a court of law, its credibility lay in its sources and in the recognizability of the facts in the testimony. Yet, despite this new research technology, H. K. Oliver, the first director of the Bureau, originally interpreted his task as one of soliciting testimony in the manner of a commission. Only after discovering that he lacked a means of circumventing the mandatory fees paid to "witnesses" did he hit upon the idea of a voluntary mail questionnaire. With this, the surveying tradition began. The political problems of satisfying diverse supporters in the fractious labor movement of the time made this resource base unstable, and, as a result, the Massachusetts bureau, under Oliver's more famous successor, Carroll Wright, sought to become something politically more stable—a kind of research organization that would collect facts on public issues and produce "balanced" reports on them.[3]

This strategy was also dependent on serving political purposes, however, and the "balanced" reports were probably no more objective, in our terms, than the advocacy research that preceded them.[4] Indeed, at this time there was no community of relevant experts, and no accepted standards for evaluating this kind of report. The few academic statisticians in colleges and universities were often highly critical of this government work, but they were dependent on government statisticians for information and, to some extent, for employment. They thus maintained cordial personal relations and tried to avoid ruptures.

THE ORIGINS OF THEORY IN SOCIOLOGY

The first generation of reformers, the direct heirs of the abolitionists, was distinctly Protestant in orientation. They believed in the efficacy of human action in bringing about the Kingdom of God on earth, in the mutability of the conditions and people who stood in the way, and in the power of persuasion. These were the premises of abolitionism, which seemed to have been vindicated by the victory of the North in the Civil War. Their continuation in the realm of the labor problem and in the other arenas proved to be fraught with many practical difficulties and considerable ambiguity. The agenda of reform was more or less fixed in the early 1870s by the early reformers, and it was an agenda that was fundamentally unchanged until the First World War. The sociologists who formed the American Sociological Society were the products of the era beginning roughly from the mid-1870s, during which the problems of reform had proven to be more difficult than anticipated. The theoretical legacy of early American sociology, and some of the distinctive problemata and themes of American sociology up to the Second World War, were fixed in this period. As a result, the problems that American sociology sought to solve were quite different from those that animated intellectuals during the development of other national sociologies.

As the American tradition in theory first developed, there was a superficial sense of consensus over sociology's theoretical mission. Early American sociologists, especially Frank Lester Ward, Albion Small, and Franklin Giddings, were nominally Comteans, at least early in their careers. True to the reformist resources on which sociology depended, they all presumed that discovery of the laws about human organization could be used for the progressive betterment of society.[5] To some extent, as had been the case for Comte, this position was taken as a means of legitimating sociology in the eyes of its reformist constituency, but much more was involved. Sociologists really believed that sociology could emulate the natural sciences; as a result, there was considerable effort to present sociology as more than mere amelioration. It was a science that could produce general theory. As Roscoe Hinkle notes:

> It was, indeed, general theory which was believed to confer academic respectability on the discipline and to prevent the field from "degenerating" into mere practical amelioration of social problems. General theory . . . sought to discover the first principles, causes, and laws of the origin, structure, and change of human association, human society, or social phenomena generically and irrespective of variant, particular, idiosyncratic, or unique forms. . . . All special (or specialized) sociology or sociologists were assumed to begin from, contribute to, and eventually return to general sociology or general theory. (1980, p. 267)

What, then, was the nature of such general theory? In general terms, early American theorists' work represents a blending of Auguste Comte's positivism with Herbert Spencer's organicism and individualism in a uniquely American combination. Comte's idea of sociology had been simple: sociology could be a science and discover the basic laws explaining the universal and invariant properties of human organization (1830-1942, pp. 5-6). For Comte, "the first characteristic of Positive Philosophy is that it regards all phenomena as subject to invariable natural *Laws*"

(p. 5, italics in original). While continental European sociologists became skeptical of this, early American sociologists embraced it, at least at a surface level, in their pronouncements. They wanted sociology to be a respectable science, and they devoted considerable space in their texts to arguing Comte's point. To be a Comtean posed a very severe problem, however, because Comte did not have a theory of human organization, save for a few rather imprecise analogies between organisms and society. Early American sociologists were thus drawn to Herbert Spencer and, to a lesser extent, Albert Schaeffle in Germany.

What emerges in early American sociology, then, are programmatic commitments to (1) a science that seeks to develop abstract general theory and (2) a combination of individualism/mentalism that is reconciled in an uneasy alliance with evolutionism, organicism, and implicit functionalism. Lester Ward's early book (1883) set the tone. It opens with a review of Comte and Spencer. In then turns to Spencer's more general cosmic theory by analyzing the process, or "law," of aggregation: primary aggregation creates matter, celestial bodies, and chemical relations; secondary aggregation generates life, organisms, humans, and mind; and tertiary aggregation creates social relations and society. Thus ends Volume I, which is 700 pages, having just established the province of sociology in relation to all other forces in the universe and the specific sciences that study these forces. After this Comtean and Spencerian "introduction," Volume II turns to sociology. Underlying Ward's characterization of other sciences and sociology is the concept of "synergy," in which the constant compounding and recompounding of energy into "cosmic creations" is the driving force of the universe (an idea that he clearly took from Spencer), and depending upon the nature of the synergetic compounding, the various sciences draw their subject matter. For Ward, then, "mind" emerges out of biotic synergy and then allows for the creation—through further compounding of energy—of social institutions that constrain and channel human energy, while at the same time allowing for the expression of ideas, feelings, and emotions. The creation of mind and intellect is the dynamic agent, or "dynamo," behind social activity. The social institutions that mind allows must achieve a balance between over- and underregulation; for the intellect that is unregulated by the organic structure of society is wasteful, whereas the overregulated intellect creates stagnation and dissolution. The optimal human condition, then, is one that allows for "telesis" or the use of disciplined intellect to mobilize the energy undergirding institutions for creative and well-understood ends.

We have left out much of the actual sociology here—that is, the institutional analysis—to emphasize the underlying metaphors in early sociological theory—evolutionism, organicism, and individualism. Humans and society evolve into organic wholes which, if operating properly, allow individuals the freedom to direct the course of future evolution (this latter argument is not Spencerian, but Comtean). Ward himself toned these ideas down considerably over the next decades, and others were to offer more scholarly, reasoned, and documented arguments. Additionally, by 1905, the major exponents of the organic analogy became disenchanted with the more literal usage of this type of reasoning (Bannister, 1987, p. 45), but the central preoccupations of what was later to become "functionalism" were well entrenched by this time.

The seeds of controversies were evident in these early theories, creating a situation where American theory began to differentiate into three distinctive strains. One is the continuation of Spencer's evolutionary approach in the work of William Graham Sumner and later Albert Keller, who, by the end of the first decade in this century, were considered to be anachronisms. Their four-volume *The Science of Society* (Sumner and Keller, 1927) represents the culmination of this tradition (we should note that Sumner's *Folkways* [1907] was originally intended to be part of *The Science of Society*, but Sumner got carried away and published it separately). *The Science of Society* was initiated in 1899, but Sumner's declining health forced him to take on his former student, Albert Keller, to complete the project. Owing to this early beginning and to Sumner's commitment to many Spencerian ideas, *The Science* looks very much like Spencer's *The Principles of Sociology*. It is filled with ethnographic and historical data; it explores both primitive and advanced patterns of social organization; and it covers about every conceivable topic as it traces the unfolding (what today we would call "differentiation") of ever more complex forms of social organization.

A second prominent approach is best personified by Charles Horton Cooley, who admitted that "nearly all of us who took up sociology between 1870, say, and 1890 did so at the instigation of Spencer" (1902, p. 263). But Cooley was quick to add that the major flaw in Spencer was his "defect of sympathy" and his tendency to conceptualize "the structure of human life . . . [as] phenomena almost wholly by analogy" (p. 266). For Cooley "the organic wholes of the social order are mental facts of much the same nature as personality, and much the same kind of sympathetic imagination is needed to grasp them" (p. 269). Social organization must be conceptualized, therefore, in terms of the mental processes that allow actors to create a "sense of common sympathy" or a "common spirit" from their face-to-face interactions (Cooley, 1909). Cooley's ideas were, of course, to be extended considerably by George Herbert Mead (1934) and later by symbolic interactionism, but the key point is that within Spencer's broad evolutionary and organicismic view, a much more mentalistic and micro sociology was being spawned in America.

Between the more macroevolutionary approach of Sumner and Keller, on the one side, and the heavily mentalistic sociology of Cooley, on the other, were intermediate approaches that accepted the organicismic view of social structure and, at the same time, stressed the importance of interpersonal sympathy and consciousness as crucial dynamics by which organic wholes are sustained. Indeed, it was common for American sociologists to define their task as one of uniting the French concern with the psychology of social life with the German tradition of institutional analysis. This more intermediate position is best represented by Franklin Giddings's work, which is heavily Spencerian, at least in its early phases, and yet highly mentalistic. Giddings's *Readings in Descriptive and Historical Sociology* (1906) highlights the duality of his approach. Much of the early part of the book describes in macro or evolutionary terms various societies; it then shifts to a more analytical discussion of population, patterns of group organization, and processes of homogeneity and differentiation of groups; next, "the social mind" is explored for several hundred pages; and, finally, the book closes with a return to more macrostructural analysis of "social organization." But some 20 years later, Giddings had begun to conceptualize social phenomena in far less than grandiose terms, signaling not only a change in his own thought but that of the profession as well. His *The Scientific Study of Human Society* (Giddings, 1924b) best illustrates this shift; here, Giddings examines "societal patterns" as "societal variables," and the methods for classifying, sampling, and assessing cause among phenomena denoted by variables are blended with older appeals for using knowledge for social telesis.

There was, then, a contradiction in early theory, but despite this contradiction, this "macroevolutionary mentalism" (if we can invent a descriptive phrase) provided a sense of intellectual unity. However, this contradiction—what would today be called "the micro versus macro" debate—was to become increasingly apparent, with most American sociologists abandoning macroevolutionary concerns by the post-World War I period. Thus, at the same time that Durkheim (Durkheim and Mauss, 1906; Durkheim, 1912) in France was supplementing his macroevolutionary and organicismic work of the 1890s (Durkheim, 1893) with an interest in the cognitive and mental underpinnings of social structure, and at the approximate period when Max Weber was defending defending *Verstehen* and writing the mentalistic opening sections of *Economy and Society*, American theorists were doing much the same thing. In France, this concern was to evolve into "structuralism," whereas in Germany it was to become more phenomenological. And in America this cognitive thrust, as reinforced by the interest in the statistical surveys that the reformist movement had inspired, was to encourage a concern with research on social action and the use of interviews, questionnaires, and statistical analyses of "attitudes," "definitions," and "orientations" of individual actors in concrete empirical settings.

Yet the conflicts of theoretical ideas among early theorists did not become evident, or at least very public, for some time, nor did the shift to empirical research occur rapidly. Part of the reason for the delay was that the lay public was receptive to grand, cosmic-sounding theories, perhaps as a substitute for the religious-reformist world views with which they had been raised. Indeed, the enormous popularity of Herbert Spencer in America at the turn of the century signals the extent to which early "theory" in sociology filled a need in the lay public for grand theorizing that seemed scientific and capable of directing reform and progress.

Another part of the reason for the masking of intellectual cleavages among early theorists resides in the fact that these theorists needed each other as a basis of mutual support for furthering their own careers and for institutionalizing sociology. The mutual support that developed among Lester Ward, Franklin Giddings, Albion Small, and Edward Ross was critical for the later organizational history of the field.

THE SEARCH FOR MATERIAL AND ORGANIZATIONAL RESOURCES IN ACADEMIA

Teaching Sociology

The creation of academic positions and departments in American sociology stands in sharp contrast to events in Europe. By 1880 in America, "sociology" or "social science" had already been taught in various universities and colleges as a substitute for the moral philosophy course that had traditionally been required of seniors (fourth-year students). Typically, this course had used Paley's *Natural Theology* as a text, but during the 1880s the process of replacing this course with "social science" or "sociology"—the terms were used interchangeably—quickened. The content of these courses was not regularized, however, nor were there any particular qualifications expected of teachers, who in the American colleges of the period taught courses in several areas and had heavy teaching loads. For virtually all the teachers of these courses, especially those who taught the course as a substitute for the traditional moral philosophy course, "sociology" was a part-time avocation. Few of these early teachers contributed to the later development of the discipline, and, generally, the courses disappeared from the curriculum when the interested faculty member left the university.

The use of textbooks in courses—a distinctly American obsession that persists to this day—greatly influenced the kind of writing and thinking that took place. The existence of a teaching canon created a demand for metatheory and synthesis, what Albion Small called "general sociology." Moreover, such metatheory could became a topic for articles and dissertations, leading to a form of conceptual analysis that successfully eliminated or discredited the key concepts of the earlier period. One of the first consequences of the systematic comparison of canonical texts was dissatisfaction with organic analogy, which had been so persuasive earlier. "Theory" thus became academicized, and theoretical writing began to take traditional academic forms.

Despite the importance of theory to the founding figures and regardless of the prestige of writing on theoretical topics in the two major Ph.D.-granting departments of this early period—Columbia University and the University of Chicago—it was not the resource base on which academic sociology rested. Rather, sociology secured a base in academia as the undefined residual category in the social sciences, a situation that allowed sociology to become responsible for reformist topics, such as charities and corrections, which had no other academic home. In a few universities, such as Yale, these topics did not become the responsibility of sociology, but elsewhere courses in these areas were crucial, especially at the graduate level, where sociology began to compete with theological training as an academic degree that served as a qualification for work in philanthropic organizations. Most graduate students at both Chicago and Columbia, particularly at the master's degree level, were interested in such careers and causes, and so the universities hired faculty to meet this demand.

For most sociology departments at both the graduate and under-graduate levels, then, one of the basic "resources" of the emerg-ing discipline was student demand for courses oriented to amel-ioration and reform.

The appeal of these courses to beginning students lay almost entirely in students' desire to do something about social evils, or in their need for self-understanding. For many early sociologists, this kind of course represented their way of understanding the village world that they were leaving. Thus the resource of student interest was dependent not only on the influence of the reform impulse but also on the power of sociology to provide self-un-derstanding to people who were living through a specific histor-ical process, namely the decline of rural and village life. Of course, as this decline continued and became normal, the audi-ence for its analysis disappeared. And, because the desire for an ideology of reform, which had served to gain an audience for Lester Ward and other early founders, was not a sufficient base of demand for a program of university study, sociology tried to secure students by converting them to the cause of "science." Indeed, this is precisely the language used in some of the auto-biographical narratives of the early sociologies, who describe their progress from their charitable impulse to a desire to under-stand the social world, and from this desire to intellectualization of the social world in "scientific" theories.

The Incorporation of Statistics

The many labor statistics bureaus, which flourished when they could secure political support through "balanced reports" or through less controversial and more routinizable data collection, proved to be inadequate instruments for reformers. The reform-ers thus sought better and more diverse instruments for es-tablishing facts. In New York, when relations between reform leaders and Columbia University were close, this desire led to support for the Department of Social Science and to the estab-lishment of Franklin Giddings' own Chair in sociology, as well as to an unusually involved set of interrelationships between the university and reform politics. Columbia thus became the major, though not the only, site for the complex interactions that developed between sociology and the major instrument of reform research, the community survey.

The community "social survey" was a research form that flourished for 25 years, from 1905 to 1930. As Robert E. Park emphasized, the social survey flourished because it met the needs of municipal reform and administration at a particular moment in the history of American cities. In his words, "the social survey movement took definite form only when two particular streams of public interest—the welfare and the efficiency movements—united" (quoted in Taylor, 1919, p. 6).

The survey movement was a large and heterogeneous affair, at a time when sociology was a small community. The Russell Sage Foundation has listed thousands of surveys performed in this period (Eaton and Harrison, 1930). The list includes many labor surveys similar to those in the early years of the labor statistics bureaus, but the list also contains other kinds of surveys, including many that were called specialized surveys, such as the 25-volume Cleveland Survey on Education (1915-1977), which was followed by an 11-volume survey on health and hospitals (1920), a 7-volume survey on recreation (1916-1920), and a survey on crime (1922). Educational surveys, concerned with such minutiae as lawn-watering practices and coal budgets, also proliferated and were supported by powerful figures in schools of education who wished to professionalize school administration. One obvious feature of most of these surveys was that they were used as a basis for some kind of governmental or institutional action or "planning." The striking feature of the survey movement, from the point of view of the problem of patronage, was that few were government sponsored; most involved the aid of the communities for which they were performed and many were undertaken entirely, or almost entirety, with volunteer help from those communities. Such help was gained because the surveys were to achieve public aims, especially the edification of the community. The dependence on local aid meant that the surveyors paid a great deal of attention to generating publicity and to enlisting the interest of the community. As a result, the surveyors stayed close to the mentality and perceptions of local professionals and to the demands of administrative rationality.

The statistical analyses done in the surveys were usually modest, and this was crucial to the utility of the surveys as means of edification.[6] This simplicity was also essential to the rapid spread of surveys, because few technical qualifications were necessary to produce visibly useful "results." The dramatic impact of the surveys was often considerable, but the contributions of the surveys to academic sociology were modest.

Yet there were other effects that were perhaps more important: academic sociologists performed some surveys and participated in many others, simultaneously learning from them and advising. Another less direct consequence was the recruitment of sociologists and the establishment of professional careers. Surveys were generally subsidized publications and thus constituted a point of entry to the professional literature for aspirants; a surprising number of persons who became academic "sociologists" in the expansion of the 1920s had started as participants in local surveys.

The Academic Compromise

Surveys nevertheless failed to find an academic home in university sociology, save in schools of agriculture. Some of the reasons for this are simple: surveying was a full-time activity, and professors needed to teach classes and direct student research. The expertise needed to perform a survey was largely organizational. There was little that a sociologist could contribute as an "expert" to the study of hospitals or recreation, and the municipal needs that these surveys addressed were administrative in character. In fact, bureaus of municipal research and professionalizing schools of social work and public administration did flourish, and these were an outgrowth of the administrative side of the survey movement. But sociologists had no specific administrative niche to occupy in public life, and they failed to develop one—a fact that haunts American sociology to this day. A more serious difficulty was integrating surveys with what already had been established as part of the academic tradition in sociology. This was a problem with two sides: (1) the problem of "the meaning" of statistics, an issue with a complex prehistory in Europe, and (2) the problem of the "scientific character" and status of sociology, a question with immediate relevance for the claims of sociology to academic respectability and a place at the table with history and economics.[7]

What happened in the face of the potential conflict over the relation between theory and statistical sociology was crucial to the history and current profile of American sociology, for the distinctive national character of American sociology stems from the compromise that reconciled the two. This reconciliation was turned into a model of research practice by Franklin Giddings at Columbia and his students, although the widespread actualization of the model did not take place until after the First World War when new funding arrangements were constructed. The difficulty of connecting theory and research was felt most acutely by Giddings from the very start of his "sociological theorizing." In essence, Giddings resurrected Comte's law of the three stages, but, following Karl Pearson, he transformed the theological, metaphysical, and positive stages to speculative, observational, and metrical. Giddings could thus resolve conceptual problems at the speculative stage, in the hope and expectation that these would be confirmed by observations and ultimately be made "metrical" (Giddings, 1901).

This kind of research—that is, theory and then empirical tests of the theory—required a quite different material base than did the reform "survey," and, most importantly, it could be performed within the limitations of time and organization of a university department. It could serve practical and academic purposes simultaneously, although it could not readily serve the purpose of edification because of the abstract character of the results. The main obstacle to the expansion of the approach was the need for statistically trained specialists. And this was an

obstacle that could not be surmounted without the organization
of sociology as an academic discipline.

The Problem of Organization

The letter of invitation to the meeting that created the American Sociological Society, which was held at the meetings of the
older American Economic Association, stated the aim of discussing "the advisability of forming a national sociological association designed to perform for sociologists services similar to those
rendered for economists by the Economic Association, and for
those interested in political science by the Political Science Association" (quoted in Stern, 1948, p. 91). The letter went on to
emphasize what was obvious to those who received it: the failure
of sociologists to organize. This failure was attributed to the fact
that "sociologists have been so largely accustomed to working
along divergent lines, and so frequently hold radically divergent
views." The letter nevertheless reasoned "that there seems to be
peculiar justification for some sort of an organization which shall
bring together at regular intervals those interested in the same
group of problems, and permit of that interchange of ideas and
comparison of projects which in other fields of knowledge has so
frequently contributed to the advancement of science" (quoted
in Stern, 1948, p. 91). And so, in 1905, the American Sociological
Society (ASS)—later to become the present-day American Sociological Association (ASA)—was formed.

Except for a group of particularly rabid and propagandistic
"Christian Sociologists," notably George Herron, the organization welcomed all who were interested in developing sociology,
and, on the eve of World War I, the organization had expanded
rapidly. By 1920, it had grown to a respectable size of about 1000
members, making it roughly equivalent in size to the American
Statistical Association, the American Political Science Association, and the American Historical Association. Figure 1.1 documents this growth. Yet, the ASS was significantly weaker than its
siblings with respect to its outlets for research publications. As is

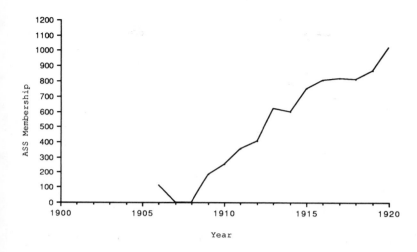

Figure 1.1. ASS Membership to 1920

the case today, many members of the society had alternative outlets for their published works and, hence, alternative bases for their prestige as scholars. For example, the American Statistical Association provided an alternative organizational base for sociologists long after the founding of the ASS, for many sociologists simply continued as members and major participants in the American Statistical Society and published in its journal rather than in the *American Journal of Sociology*. The *Journal* was made the official research outlet of the ASS, but in many ways it remained the house organ of Chicago sociology and was viewed with derision and suspicion by many in the field.

The organizational achievement of creating a sociological society was nevertheless remarkable in view of the fact that, unlike the situation of other professional organizations, the number of persons with academic degrees in sociology was still very small. As Figure 1.2 documents, only about 20 doctoral degrees were being granted per annum by the end of World War I, and this fact meant that the proportion of members in the society holding

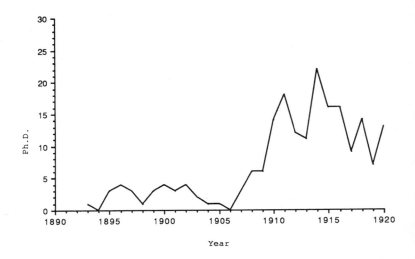

Figure 1.2. Sociology Ph.D.'s until 1920

Ph.D.'s in sociology was small. The other social sciences, with a
longer history of Ph.D. production and in many cases a higher
level of production, were not so dependent on members with
minimal training, although these too had a high proportion of
members who were neither academics nor professionally trained.

As we will come to see, these irregularities in the growth of the
Ph.D.-holding core of the discipline were to have significant
demographic consequences for the discipline. This early generation of Ph.D.'s was to hold the major offices in the society for the
whole of the period between World Wars I and II. The retirement
or death of almost all of the founders by 1930 meant that young
Ph.D.'s took charge of the ASS, and the fact that the production
of Ph.D.'s in the decade from 1914 to 1924 was irregular meant
that they held these positions longer. Moreover, when they retired in the 1940s, a new set of vacancies created opportunities
for a dramatic change in the leadership of American sociology.

CONCLUSION

In the early years, the material, symbolic, and organizational resources available to sociologists were limited and often contradictory. The material resource base for sociology initially came from the reformist movement, and it is on this base that the first sociologists could conduct empirical research and find an audience for their writings. The sense that sociology could be useful for solving "social evils" provided legitimating symbols in the lay community, but it often made academic sociology a residual discipline that took the ameliorative leftovers from other fields. Moreover, the efforts to unify sociology symbolically with a theoretical scientism revolving around positivism, organicism, evolutionism, and interventionism proved to be an uneasy state of affairs. Efforts at unification under the banner of science were often at odds with the reformist material base on which early sociology existed inside and outside of academia. Private funds for research, student interest and enrollments, and public support of municipal surveys all depended upon maintaining a close connection between social problems and sociological analysis. Eventually, theory would seem remote from these problems, and the surveys increasingly lost much of their moral impact and capacity for public edification.

It is with this resource base—shaky both symbolically and materially—that American sociology sought to mobilize its organizational resources. The formation of the American Sociological Society in 1905 represented an uneasy compromise. Intellectual differences were suppressed in the name of forging a professional discipline. While some unity could be found in theories—positivism, organicism, and evolutionism—and in research methods—surveys and tabular presentations—these intellectual currents were not sufficient to produce a professional organization with great capacity to control the destiny of sociology. For as the material base of the discipline was to change, so did the fragile theoretical and, to a lesser extent, methodological consensus. Indeed, as the decades of this century passed, the

diversity of the field, which had been glossed over by the founders, was to become increasingly apparent.

NOTES

1. In some cases, the disagreements led to the creation of splinter political
parties led by figures in the reform movement who had made reputations in the
Civil War, such as Benjamin Butler of Massachusetts. Butler had redistributed
wealth while military governor in New Orleans (and allegedly indulged a
penchant for silver spoons, earning him the sobriquet "Spoons") and was
relieved of his command. Yet he was elected to Congress in time to serve as one
of the managers in the impeachment of Andrew Johnson, and then made a series
of races for higher office, including one as presidential candidate for the Green-
back-Labor and Anti-monopoly parties in 1884. The failure of the splinter
parties, none of which was able to obtain a national base, was one reason that
reformers directed their efforts into issue-oriented organizations rather than
party politics. These reform organizations succeeded in part because they did
not demand the exclusive loyalty of their followers (as labor unions and political
parties did). Indeed, the directorates of the various reform organizations, the
readership of their publications, and their aims tended to overlap a great deal.
2. Arthur Vidich and Stanford Lyman, *American Sociology* (1985), give an
elaborate demonstration of the religious roots of American sociological thinking, a theme that no account of the history of American sociology can neglect.
In our discussion, the religious heritage will figure as a resource: a motivation
for persons to become sociologists or support sociological work.
3. Massachusetts had been the first state to establish a full-fledged geologi-
cal survey, and the pattern was imitated and modified by many other states, and
finally taken up by the federal government. Such was also the case for labor
statistics. Ultimately most of the states established some kind of analogous
bureau, as did several European countries. None of the other state bureaus,
however, engaged in the range of social research performed by the Massachusetts survey.
4. The questions on the "blanks" of the questionnaires used by the Massachusetts bureau were, by modern standards, badly worded, and the lists of
questions were very long. Many of the questions called for quite simple numer-
ical answers about the number of persons employed and the like, but many were
requests for opinions—and not simple questions of approval or disapproval of
some statement or approximation, but complex questions about the respon-
dent's belief in the causes of various undesirable features of the contemporary
situation, such as the high price of provisions. Few workers or employers
proved to be willing to answer the complete list of questions; most simply failed
to respond. The answers of those who did were generally "curt and unsatisfactory" (Bureau of Statistics of Labor [Massachusetts], 1870, p. 23). The bureau did
follow up, with correspondence, on responses that it found "strange or unmean-
ing" (p. 12), but apparently not to improve the response rate. In one of these

early surveys, the "circular" or questionnaire addressed to workers contained 137 questions and was sent to 268 workers, of whom 114 replied. When possible, unskilled laborers who were not literate enough to complete a blank were interviewed orally. The equally demanding circular for employers, also sent with a prepaid envelope, received only 217 relies out of 1248. The bureau was well aware of the inadequacy of the formulations of questions they were asking. In the first report they quote Rousseau to the effect that "the art of asking questions . . . is the art of masters rather than of scholars, and one must have learnt many things to know how to ask about a thing one does not understand" (Bureau of Statistics of Labor [Massachusetts], 1870, p. 16). This was used to justify the effort the bureau spent on gaining background, and especially historical information. In the 50 years of the bureau's activity, the means of asking questions improved, though the same kinds of "opinion" questions, requiring a great deal of inference on the part of the respondents and treating them as experts with special insight into such topics as the causes of high prices of provisions, were asked into the 20th century.

The bureau had no alternative other than to refine its methods within its legal limitations. One of Wright's first actions in office was to test the method of mailing questionnaires by sending them to clergymen, who, he supposed, should be responsible and literate enough to reply. Of 1530 mailed, only 544 were returned, several of which were blank, others "sneeringly express[ing] the intimation that what we were asking was none of our business" (Bureau of Statistics of Labor [Massachusetts], 1874, p. 24). Wright abandoned the mail method, except for certain infrequent uses, and relied on personal interviews, especially visits to employers to examine their records, which produced much better cooperation. Much of the work of the bureau was secondary analysis, especially of data on wages, but a great deal of data was collected by "special agents" of the bureau conducting interviews. These interviews were governed by the interviewer's understanding of the objects of the inquiry rather than by adherence to any elaborate interviewing procedure, and this was understood to be one of the reasons for the superiority of the personal interview: Wright later explained that the questions on mailed blanks, no matter how precisely formulated, tended to be interpreted differently by different respondents, and the resulting data were therefore inferior to the results obtained by personal interviews.

5. Dirk Kaesler's *Soziologische Abenteuer* (1985) describes the process of converting ameliorative goals of students into a concern for theory. In the case of E. E. Eubank, a missionary's son who went to the Chicago sociology department to learn about how to better aid the poor, the transformation was complete: he left a reverent student of the European "makers" of theory. The same story is told repeatedly in other life-histories. John Gillin, one of Giddings's students whose placement at Ross's department at Wisconsin was pivotal to the expansion of the Columbia approach, recalled that he had first been exposed to the idea of "sociology" through the powerful preaching of Herron as a student at the Iowa College at Grinnell, where Herron was Professor of Applied Christianity. One of his courses, Gillin later recalled, was called Christian Sociology, the other Sociology. The message was still fresh in Gillin's mind 30 years later: "This presentation of Christianity gave wings to my youthful imagination and

provided a rational outlet for my evangelical enthusiasm. Up to that time
Christianity for me had meant believing certain doctrines about things; the only
practical outlet for it here and now was the negative one of controlling one's
own passions and impulses and trying to convert one's fellow creatures to
Christianity. In Herron an entirely new direction was given to Christian purpose. Here were social evils contrary to the spirit of Christ. Christianity, in his
presentation, was a challenge to those evils. These evils constituted a call to the
individual Christian personally to help to cure them. The goal of every man's
Christian purpose was not merely to save his own soul, but to save society"
(Gillin, BPUC, pp. 5-6). Gillin in fact did go on to become a pastor in a country
church, and his sensitization to the social consequences of action made him
intensely curious about such matters as the ways in which the church elders
regulated marriage and the ways the youth of the community managed to
escape their control. This community was to become the subject of his M.A.
thesis at Columbia. But his journey to Columbia sociology was not direct. He
decided to leave his pastorate and go to Union Seminary in New York, with the
aim of learning more about applying Christianity to social problems. He enrolled in Giddings's course on the evolution of society while finishing his
divinity degree, and ultimately stayed to complete his degrees in sociology,
writing a notable "community study" dissertation on the Dunkers.

Gillin wrote that "the events which directed my feet into the paths of
sociology and away from the Ministry . . . may appear to be quite adventitious"
and reflected that "looking back over those years I see that my intellectual
curiosity was always dominant over my feeling." But the supremacy was never
complete. "With the years my intellectual curiosity . . . I find has become linked
to that old desire to solve some of society's problems" (Gillin, BPUC, p. 11). This
was the theme of a whole generation of Giddings's students as well as Small's.
We shall see some of the consequences of the pattern of recruitment into the
discipline that is typified by Gillin in the 1930s as this generation comes into
control of the discipline. For the moment, we need to consider the constraints
of recruitment and reproduction. However much persons like Giddings and
Small ridiculed or objected to the "Christian Sociology" of a Herron, they were
nonetheless dependent on these figures for attracting students into graduate
programs in sociology. There were other sources, but they were meager. Giddings managed to attract some students from cognate fields, such as Odum, who
received a Ph.D. in psychology from G. Stanley Hall at Clark and was exposed
to Giddings's (1896) *Principles* in a course taught by Giddings's student Frank
Hamilton Hankins. But the largest number of potential recruits in this period
before the elective system was fully established in American colleges and before
the wide distribution of sociologists in undergraduate institutions was in the
schools of divinity.

To abandon this body of potential recruits, as Small understood, would be
self-destructive of sociology as a program of graduate study. Indeed, these
necessities of recruitment concerned Small from his earliest discussions with
Ward, while Small was still at Colby College. In 1880, when Small introduced
Ward's ideas to students in a course intended to replace "moral philosophy," he
suppressed Ward's antireligious statements, and he encouraged Ward himself
to moderate them. Ward's reply was caustic: I "did not write for the feeble-

minded" (quoted in Stern, 1933, p. 165). Small's remonstrations reflected a concern that Ward did not share, the concern of a teacher presenting material that students would readily reject or ignore. Yet the processes by which recruitment took place were delicate, and the recruitments often were, as Gillin said, adventitious. On the one hand, the maintenance of these processes required sociology departments to have faculty who appealed to the audience attracted by the practical side of the social gospel, persons like Vincent, or to preserve such ties as the lucky arrangement Columbia had by which students at Union Seminary, at the time one of the largest minsterial training centers of the world, could take courses and be converted from theology to sociology. In fact, these "paths" were quite carefully maintained, and Giddings, himself a rebellious son of a Congregational minister, was personally well suited to the task of conversion.

6. Throughout the 19th century, "moral statisticians" in Europe had struggled, ultimately unsuccessfully, with the problems of giving a causal interpretation to the relationships between the rates recorded by official statisticians (Porter, 1986, pp. 151-192, 240-255). This tradition was the original source for Mayo-Smith who continued to believe in the ultimate scientific significance and potential of social statistics after disillusionment had set in among many of the Europeans. Sociology could compete with this tradition (as it did in Germany by the drawing of a sharp line between "pure sociology" and statistics), or incorporate it, or be incorporated by it. Small's and Vincent's text (1894) solved the problem of the empirical content of sociology by the use of a rubric congenial to the organicist content of the theory, a solution that could not be readily extended to the topic of the relationship between statistical rates. Mayo-Smith was quite clear about the conflict and sensitive to the problems involved. The style and claims of Mayo-Smith's major "sociological" work, titled *Statistics and Sociology* (1910), are indicative not only of his and his students' views, but of the status of social statistics on the eve of the methodological work of Giddings and his determined assimilation of the philosophical message of Karl Pearson. The source material is the same as that of the moral statisticians, namely census material as well as vital and criminal statistics. The organization of the chapters, however, follows a novel formal scheme, including sections titled Sociological Purpose, Statistical Data, Scientific Tests, and Reflective Analysis (Mayo-Smith, 1895, p. vi). The book begins with a chapter on the service of statistics to sociology, which is defined as "the science which treats of social organization," and which "has for object of research the laws which seem to underlie the relations of men in society." By "law" Mayo-Smith says he means "the ordinary empirical law, namely the necessary connection which subsists between a phenomenon and the conditions under which that phenomenon exists," in this case "the facts of social organization and the way those facts are related to one another." If by "synthesis" of these empirical laws we are able to "detect the goal toward which changes in social organization seem to be leading . . . we have a philosophy of society . . . which is also sometimes called sociology." But "the fundamental thing . . . is the study of . . . the facts of social organization from which such a synthesis must be composed" (1910, p. 1). This defines a relationship between the descriptive laws that statistics arrives at and the kinds of topics that were part of Spencer's, and of Ward's, evolutionism and claims

"fundamental" status for descriptive empirical laws. Nothing is said to discredit the possibility of such a synthesis, other than by labeling it "philosophy," which at the time was not a pejorative term. "Sociology," he continues, "has not yet reached that stage of development where the discovery of some great central truth enables us to change from the inductive to the deductive method" (p. 2). But matters are, he acknowledges, rather worse than that. Even if we accept these premises, we are faced with "two great difficulties,—one is the enormous number and complexity of the social phenomena to be described; the second is the lack of any precise means of measuring or gauging social forces, that is, of estimating the degree of intensity in the relations of social phenomena with one another" (p. 3). Past sociologists have, he thinks, made some bad choices in the face of complexity. One is to take "all history, all archaeology, all observations of travelers, as material for their science, and have treated all of this material as equally valuable," but Mayo-Smith finds it impossible to believe that all of this material is equally valuable. Because accepting it all as equally valuable makes the problem of empirical sociology "unmanageable," we must make a choice. The choice he recommends is based on a choice about the proximate goals of sociology: to seek "simple relations of cause and effect, of coexistence and of sequence" and to abandon "artificial classification . . . based on biological analogies," specifically the organic analogies of Spencer and Schaeffle, which explain nothing. We need to "define with some precision the range of phenomena which furnish the material for Sociology, and the method by which this material should be treated so as to enable us to measure social forces. If we can do this, we shall escape the danger of being overwhelmed by the multiplicity of phenomena and avoid the cheap and unsatisfactory makeshift of an explanation of superficial analogies" (pp. 5-6).

The antinomies in this argument are worth stressing: between statistical data and all other kinds, between laws and analogies, and between the immediate and the distant aims of sociology. The necessity to choose some restricted range of data is dictated by the problem of complexity. But it is unclear why statistical data are any more likely to lead to results than any other kind of data. What statistics can do, Mayo-Smith argues, is "to direct our attention to possible relations of cause and effect" and to enable us to measure the degree of effect and identity differences in impact (1910, p. 15). This knowledge is "the only basis for the possibility of social reform" (p. 16). And this in turn can serve "to predicate the existence of social laws." He concedes that there is a rather large gap between statistical results and "laws," but he insists that statistics "helps us on our way" to this goal. In any case, he argues, "We are surrounded by sociological or social problems which urgently demand solution. We cannot wait for the completed science; we must seek to understand the conditions affecting the particular problem before us" (p. 16).

7. Behind this was a more fundamental dispute over the nature of explanation. A reviewer of the *Principles* in *The Nation* had explained that the aim of science was to trace phenomena to true causes (Bannister, 1987, p. 21). The *vera causa* tradition, to which Ward closely hewed, continued to form a problem-focus for critics in the interwar years. Giddings, like Pearson, rejected this tradition, which was adhered to by few, if any, sophisticated commentators on science by the end of the 19th century. But it was a tradition with a distinguished

intellectual lineage, and it was there to express the disquiet that scientists as well as social scientists had with the more extreme formulations of Pearson and Mach on cause, a concept that Pearson denounced as a metaphysical and animistic survival from a prior stage of intellectual development (Pearson, 1900; cf. Giddings, 1922, pp. 127-143). This resolution was not accepted everywhere. Small derided Giddings's views. In 1901 he wrote to Ward as follows: "Giddings' last book [*Inductive Sociology*, 1901] nonpluses me. He has a wonderful facility of 'subjective interpretation,' and there is a certain sort of stimulus about it, but I think it would relieve me to utter agnosticism about the whole business [i.e., sociology] if I thought that sort of thing was real sociology. 'It is and cannot come to good' is the only verdict I can pass. . . . Two or three of our physical science men have looked it over and they pronounce it absolute drivel. I don't believe it is as bad as that . . . I sized it up as a somewhat stimulating condiment, but a starvation diet if it comprises the bulk of the bill of fare" (quoted in Stern, 1937, pp. 305-306). In the same letter, Small reports that Ross offered to review the book and was apparently more enthusiastic than Small. He later writes that he "had a long talk with Ross" and that "he thinks himself that he somewhat overdid the professional courtesy business with Giddings" (quoted in Stern, 1937, p. 306), a clear example of Small's concern with the nuances of praise.

TWO

The Focused Replaces the Grand: American Sociology During the Interwar Years

From the perspective of the younger sociologists, the intellectual development of sociology was revived after the First World War. In 1929, Jessie Bernard made the following observation:

> About 1918, the barren years came to an end and the present efflorescence in sociology began. Mention need be made only of Cooley's *Social Process*, Thomas and Znaniecki's *The Polish Peasant*, Ross's *Principles of Sociology*, Park and Burgess' *Introduction to the Science of Sociology*, Ogburn's *Social Change*, Bernard's *Instinct*, Giddings' *Studies in the Theory of Human Society*, Sumner and Keller's *Science of Society*, the establishment of [the journal] *Social Forces*, and the inauguration of the community studies at the University of Chicago. . . . (J. Bernard, 1929, p. 48)

The last two of these developments and the publication of *The Polish Peasant* (Thomas and Znaniecki, 1918) were the result of the new resources that sociology was beginning to secure from foundations and philanthropists. The publication of the Park and Burgess'(1924), as well as Ross's, texts signified the expansion of the competitive textbook market. The others signified the break-up and transformation of the remaining fragments of the theoretical views that had been shared, with many quiet reservations, by the founding generation. *The Science of Society* (1927), based on Sumner's ideas but turned by his student Albert Keller in an evolutionary direction, served as the basic text for a heterodox tradition at Yale. In fact, Keller refused to use the term *sociology* or to participate in the American Sociological Society (ASS). Bernard's (1924) *Instinct* was a behavioristic critique of a concept that was paradigmatic of the older style of theorizing, and this work was a herald of a new relation to psychology. Cooley's (1918) *Social Process* was concerned with the interactional character of those processes discussed in the older texts. Giddings's last theory book (1922), a collection of essays, and Ogburn's major work (1922) represented the passing of the generational torch in the Columbia tradition.

The differences in these last two texts typify the change. Franklin Giddings was centrally concerned with the lag between material conditions and collectively shared ideas, but he theorized about this lag as a part of a general conception of the selective processes behind social evolution. In contrast, Ogburn made "cultural lag" into a much narrower problem to be addressed "empirically" and independently of any grand cosmic scheme. This shift from the grand to the more focused became the hallmark of the decade. In part, this was in response to changes in the sources of patronage for sociology. The emergence of foundations, and especially the Rockefeller family foundations, as a major source of financial support for academic social science had major consequences during the 1920s. Sociology shared in these funds, and the new organizational structures created to secure and distribute them had significant effects on the discipline.

One aim of the Rockefeller officers was to make social science "realistic," and the differential support of various kinds of social science that conformed to that vague goal had an enormous influence on the careers and reputations of those sociologists who conformed to its dictates. Ultimately, this initiative by the Rockefeller foundations produced a revolt in the name of the old "Wardian" conception of a social science devoted to public edification, and, while that revolt failed, it altered the boundaries of the discipline and certified a new core disciplinary elite, with distinctive and narrow intellectual allegiances.

In this chapter and the one that follows, then, we will consider the changes in the resource base for sociology by examining a series of arrangements under which sociology was funded. These funds were, of course, not the only resource sociologists had, for direct appeal to public audiences, student demand, professional organizations and journals, and internal distribution of reputations all continued to be features of disciplinary life. But each of these was affected by the new modes of financing.

MATERIAL RESOURCES AND THE PROFESSIONALIZATION OF THE SURVEY MOVEMENT

The Institute for Social and Religious Research

The quantitatively most sophisticated large-scale sociological research of the early part of the interwar period was carried out by John D. Rockefeller, Jr.-supported Institute for Social and Religious Research (ISRR), originally called the Committee on Social and Religious Surveys. The research program of this institute evolved out of a failure of an even more ambitious attempt to extend the older volunteer-labor "survey" model to the study of the church as an institution.[1] The objective of the Interchurch World Movement, founded in early 1919 and based on the model of prewar studies in Vermont of the rural churches of Windsor County, was to survey every evangelical church in America. In the summer of 1920 the movement collapsed, but only after data on thousands of churches had been collected. The ISRR finished some of the work of the Interchurch World Movement and took on the task of analyzing the data that had been collected under its auspices. The ISRR also resurveyed as a check on the data.[2]

The leash was always kept tight by Rockefeller, for "at no time . . . did he contemplate endowing the enterprise, and his annual contributions to it were made with no assurance of indefinite continuance" (Fisher, 1934, p. 7). Although "there was never a trace of interference or dictation by [the board] after a project had been authorized," the board and staff were quite aware that "Mr. Rockefeller, Jr., based the amount of his yearly donation partly on the appeal which the specific projects proposed for the ensuing year made to him" (Fisher, 1934, p. 15).[3] The cage, however, was golden. The grants were substantial and were sufficient to employ a full-time research staff, usually of about 45 persons, who worked in a team fashion on the projects. These included several figures who were later to be important in social research, such as Lawrence Frank, Luther Fry, and Robert Lynd.

When the organization was renamed in 1922, the aims established were practical: to "increase the effectiveness for good of the social and religious forces of the world, especially those of Protestant Christianity" by promoting cooperation and the economical use of resources (the goals of the older survey movement as blended with the efficiency movement) and "by bringing to the tasks to be accomplished the help of scientific inquiry, accurate knowledge, and broad horizon" (Fisher, 1934, p. 8). In seeking money from Rockefeller, then, the basic issue for researchers was clear: define a position within which "science" and rather vague "practical" aims could be reconciled.[4]

The Rockefeller advisors included some trained social scientists, including the sociologist George Vincent, the psychologist Beardsley Ruml, and the economist and statistician E. E. Day. Their ideas were combined with those of the Rockefeller Foundation about the nature of science. From the point of view of the academics with whom they dealt, these ideas were not very specific. The Rockefeller charities generally supported what they called "realistic" studies and rejected what they regarded as pure academicism, theory, and moralizing—though they supported what they regarded as worldly Christian social action of a practical kind. But it was left to the academics to fit their ideas about the nature of social science to these broad notions.[5]

The external form of many of the "sociological" books published under ISRR sponsorship was realistic in the sense of being highly statistical, with one of the factions in the staff equating "scientific" and "statistical".[6] In the case of Luther Fry's dissertation (1924), for instance, the book contained 42 tables, 20 charts, and 5 maps, and reported a number of Pearsonian correlations.[7] The premise of the ISRR, as reflected in Fry's dissertation, was "that it was impossible to understand the functioning of any church without a knowledge of its social and economic environment" (1924, p. xi).[8] This concern with "external forces" came to influence the Christian education research done by the ISRR. Whereas the first study paid little attention to the social origins of seminary students or to "environmental factors conditioning the functioning of the church, . . . the second study, 11 years later, give detailed attention to both these matters" (Fisher, 1934, p. 18). The term *function* was a convenient one, because it was Spencerian and therefore "sociological," yet practical, in the sense it had been employed in the various "efficiency" campaigns that had been associated with the earlier survey movement. In Fry's conclusion the correlational results are treated causally: "environmental" conditions, such as economic circumstances, were found to affect all aspects of a church's life; population density, for example, increased attendance. Fry's final section concerned itself with generational change in the churches of Windsor County, Vermont, and found that no church decline—the issue that motivated the original effort—had actually taken place.

The twin themes of "change" and "external causes" were the centerpiece of the most famous of the ISRR studies, which began in 1923 and eventuated in *Middletown* (Lynd and Lynd, 1929). The study was understood by its sponsors to be a continuation of the kind of work done by Fry and Brunner, the leader of the team that produced the very expensive and highly quantitative American village study that had stressed partial and multiple correlation analysis. *Middletown* was later described by the administrator of the ISRR as "a pioneer attempt at a much wider correlation" tracing them over a generation and showing "the interrelations of all aspects of life and institutions in a small city" (Fisher, 1934,

p. 18). It was also a pure product of the ISRR internal funding system: the researcher who fell heir to the project, Robert Lynd, was a young divinity school graduate who was assistant director of the religious education department of the ISRR. The work also illustrates the transition from volunteer to professional surveys.[9] One of the directors of the ISRR, Shelby Harrison, who had been director of a traditional reform survey of Springfield, Illinois, hoped that the religious leaders of those communities studied would be involved in formulating the study. Instead, Lynd performed the research in Muncie, Indiana, with his wife, three assistants, the help of the ISRR technical staff, and the advice of various professional sociologists.

To contemporary academics, this kind of structure was threatening: a committee of the American Association of University Professors expressed concern over "the tendency to organize research and provide for its support through extra-academic foundations, societies, and industrial plants" (quoted in Ogg, 1928, p. 113). But the anxieties did not prove to be well founded, and the fate of the ISRR in the 1930s served as an object lesson for the social sciences. The story of *Middletown* is revealing because it shows the extent to which the statistically oriented researchers of the ISRR had overestimated the strength of their position.

The project itself had a stormy history in the Institute, in large part because of its formlessness. When the manuscript was finally submitted, Lynd was told that it was unpublishable. Although it was the practice of the ISRR to subsidize publication, the staff thought the manuscript was uninteresting and irreligious. But the methodological issue, the degree to which the core technical staff valued nonstatistical work, was crucial in their rejection of the manuscript. Lynd, who was adept at using New York networks, had taken a job at the Commonwealth Fund and a position as Wesley Claire Mitchell's assistant at the Social Science Research Counsel (SSRC), another Rockefeller-supported operation. He did not give up on the manuscript, and after gaining the support of Clark Wissler, an anthropologist who was important in New York foundation circles and who promised to write an introduction, he secured permission from the ISRR to publish it on his own (something the ISRR leaders assured him was impossible). He then showed the manuscript to Harcourt, a major publisher, which accepted it with extensive cuts. The book became a bestseller, and Lynd himself became an important public figure. Columbia, after requiring some token course work, granted him a Ph.D. and appointed him to the sociology department.

Of more immediate interest is the fate of the ISRR. The work of the Institute was the most advanced and massive effort at statistical sociology in history; prior efforts may have had more data, but never had so much effort been put into the use of sophisticated analytic efforts. The researchers were proud of their work, even arrogant, if the rejection of the *Middletown* episode is any indication. To their astonishment, Rockefeller told the Institute in 1932 that his support would cease and an agreement was reached to finish five projects then in progress. Foundations fund in cycles, and disenchantment with the program after 10 years is not unusual, but the situation of the ISRR was different. The work was a personal interest of John D. Rockefeller, Jr., not a program director's project. What the destruction of the ISRR showed was that the work had never proved itself in the eyes of Mr. Rockefeller and his ever-present advisors, and this suggested that there was, in fact, no constituency for statistical social science and no overwhelming practical value to the sophisticated forms of analysis that the ISRR had so assiduously pursued. Moreover, the total dependence on the whims of Rockefeller was another object lesson. The same kinds of lessons were to be given to the SSRC and the University of Chicago, two other Rockefeller dependencies, at about the same time. But in neither case was the result so simple.

The Chicago School and Empirical Research

The Local Community Research Committee (LCRC) grant to the University of Chicago and the supplementary grants and the grants establishing the SSRC that followed were based largely on the influence of a single person: Robert Merriam, a political scientist trained in the 1890s at Columbia.[10] Sociology was a major beneficiary of the Rockefeller grants to social science at Chicago, though that was not the primary interest of the Rockefeller funders. Like the ISRR grant, the one establishing the LCRC at Chicago was something between a proposal grant and a no-strings block grant for social science research, but it differed in several respects. The ISRR grant was for a research shop organized on a team basis; the LCRC grant was an attempt to reorient a thriving academic program in the social sciences by the use of subsidies for selected classes of activity. The relationship between the Rockefeller family and the University of Chicago was unique, because this university was the family's special interest (having been founded with Rockefeller money). As a result, the total amount of funding was exceptionally high, but the fact of funding was not exceptional, since less restrictive but smaller grants to social science research were made to a number of universities in the 1920s.

The figure who dominated sociology's contribution to the LCRC was Robert Ezra Park. His academic background was in philosophy, and he had worked as a journalist for The Congo Reform Association and as a factotum for Booker T. Washington. Park had developed his sociological ideas in the teens; he began to correspond with W. I. Thomas in 1913, moved to Chicago, and gradually became a central figure in the aging Chicago department, moving from summer school instructor to full-time faculty member in 1919. Park was a distinctive intellect, but it was something of an accident that his ideas became as important as they did. The department might have gone in a quite different direction in the early 1920s, but the LCRC was established at a time when the sociology department was in a plastic state. It had lost most of its early members to death, departure, or promotion to administrative positions and had not recovered from the severe trauma of W. I. Thomas's forced resignation in 1918.

The sociology department was virtually a blank slate at the time Park became a full member of the faculty, and the LCRC grant enabled Park to create a new kind of sociology at Chicago.

Two features characterized it: (1) a distinctive research ethic, and (2) a novel relationship to the older reform tradition. These were each successfully transmitted to students, but in a manner that depended very much on Park's personal charisma as well as socialization into the community created by the LCRC. The community itself was made possible by the fact that a significant source of research funds was locally controlled. Control was also centralized: projects had to fit the larger aims of the grant and receive the support of influential members of the Chicago faculty. Thus Park had an exceptionally powerful position, and, although the LCRC grant was controlled by an interdisciplinary committee, he had a high degree of influence over the distribution of the funds within sociology, without the burden of direct scrutiny such as existed at the ISRR. The role of Merriam as intermediary, and the secondary role of sociology in the grant as a whole, meant that Park did not need to justify his approach in detail to the Rockefeller representatives—something that involved much of the time and effort of other recipients of Rockefeller funds, such as Howard Odum of North Carolina. Nonetheless, the work done by Park fit the Rockefeller agenda in important respects. The focus of the research conducted by the LCRC was "realistic" in the requisite sense, and the problems it addressed were almost invariably problems that had long histories in the reformist movements of the prewar period.

The appeal of Park's sociology to students was also crucial. Chicago sociology, like other graduate programs at the time, began with new graduate students who were motivated by a desire to solve social problems. Park transformed the reform sentimentality of these students, often brutally, into an equally intense commitment to a distinctive kind of sociological curiosity. Capturing in a few phrases the transformation of subject matter that Park and his colleagues accomplished is difficult, because the attitudes of the older reform movements that the Rockefeller almoners pushed in the direction of "realism" are alien to present sensibilities. For example, one of the famous studies of the Chicago school was Paul Cressey's study of the taxi-dance hall (1932), in which "dancers" engaged in various mildly erotic activities with paying customers under the guise of ballroom dancing. Precisely this kind of "unwholesome" activity was a major concern of the enlightened reformers in the prewar period, but the character of this concern had taken the form of a strange mixture of Puritanism and naive faith in the power of regulation. Cressey's study approached the emotionally loaded topic of sexual amusements not merely in the unbiased, "objective" manner of a statistical analyst, but in a way that made this subject matter a legitimate topic for sympathetic understanding without moral horror.[11]

The importance of this transformation of the subject matter, and the consequent gain in access to the "problems," was enormous, particularly from the point of view of the recruits to the Chicago sociology. They went through a transformation away from "do-gooderism" to something akin to intellectual voyeurism.[12] In contrast, Giddings-sponsored studies at Columbia were characteristically organized around explicit theoretical ideas, which were to be put through the three stages of scientificization, with the ultimate goal being "metricization," however distant.

But Park was concerned with substance of a particular kind. If we recall the work of the Bureau of Statistics of Labor (Massachusetts), which generally began with a dispute or conflict in public opinion or perception that it sought to adjudicate, we can see why Park and his students believed themselves to be doing something more fundamental. Consider his description of his work on the Oriental problem:

> Previous investigations on the coast have sought primarily to determine the merits of the issues raised by the presence of the Oriental; that is, to arbitrate and adjudicate the disputed questions. This study . . . has sought primarily to learn—irrespective of their merits—how these issues actually arose, what were their sources in the social situations themselves, in the experiences of individual men and women, in human nature generally, and in the existing state of mind. (quoted in Matthews, 1977, p. 114)

This was a kind of sociology of knowledge—interpreting meanings and attitudes in the local experiences that formed them. It was also a general strategy: sociology, as Park says in the first chapter of Park and Burgess (1924), "has to do with those modifications in human beings that are due to the human environment" (quoted in Raushenbush, 1979, p. 82).

These formulations are striking for their vagueness; Park taught sociology by example and eschewed both formal statements of methodology and theory.[13] Thus, the model was not readily transmitted as either a theoretical or methodological doctrine; at Chicago, it was taught through immersion and osmosis. And the experience of performing research under the eyes of a community with a shared sense of the distinctive character of the sociological enterprise, and with an experiential sense of having made sociological discoveries, made immersion a most satisfying form of intellectual and emotional life. From the point of view of the resource base for sociology within the university, the significant consequence of Park's model was that it provided an identity for its adherents *as sociologists* and, in the process, preserved some of the original naive motivations with which students began their studies. Indeed, in some cases, the element of the romanticization of the downtrodden and stigmatized became a basic element of their new identities.

The arrival at Chicago of William F. Ogburn and the statistical orientation from Columbia in 1928 meant that some kind of accommodation between the doctrinal conception of sociology as a metrical "science" and the Parkian sense of sociology as an approach to substantive problems would need to be developed. In the early 1930s, a political accommodation within the department did develop. Personal relations between the students of Park and Ogburn, together with a de-emphasis on Ogburn's part of the theoretical implications of Giddings's vision of sociology as a science, meant that a loose working consensus did arise in the early 1930s. A "Chicago" identity that bridged various styles of sociological research work developed and proved to be relatively attractive to students through the 1930s, after the LCRC grant ended. Thus "Chicago sociology" was sufficiently in demand by students that the department was capable of functioning as a large academic program even with levels of grant support that were greatly diminished from those in the 1930s.

Chicago's model of sociology—an academic culture in a department with many students and a vital *gemeinschaftliche* ambiance—was not readily generalizable to the broader discipline or to other departmental situations. As a result, the emergence of a distinctive Chicago achievement also marked the beginning of a culturally divided discipline—one in which not only are theoretical and methodological topics disputed but also in which separate and virtually autonomous forms of intellectual life exist. Like the other subcultures that developed in the 1930s, Chicago systematically excluded much of what had previously passed for sociology. The sentimental Christianity that marked many of the early Chicago Ph.D.'s was only part of what was excluded; much of the conceptual analysis favored by Small's students disappeared as well. And there was a sharp generational division, and in some cases a strong antagonism, between "Chicago" sociologists of the old type and the new Chicagoans.

Where the Chicago model failed was in securing a base of funding support. There was no substantial continuing market for its research in either government or the foundations, nor was this sort of activity the kind that could be supported as a literary activity through sales to the public. The value of the sociological viewpoint developed by Park for the solution of problems on the public agenda was real, but limited. The public in Chicago was aware of the work in the department, and Park successfully cultivated some support from civic leaders, but attempts to translate the insights of the Chicago school into practice—as in the case of a program designed to reduce delinquency—had little impact because of the imprecise nature of the proposed "solutions." Long before these efforts to prove the utility of the work were made, the Rockefeller supporters of the Chicago enterprise, who had never had any special affection for the work done by the sociology department, were expressing their disappointment at the failure of their funding policy to produce the intended effect.

The grants of the 1920s had been designed to wean scholars from their interest in purely scholarly concerns, which the officers of the foundations ridiculed as merely a stage or phase in the process of developing disciplines with methods that could produce applicable social knowledge (Fosdick, 1952; also see Matthews, 1977, p. 112). Beardsley Ruml, writing in 1930, complained that the last stage had not been reached quickly enough, and he called for research that led in the "direction of social technology—or social engineering—with its recognized divisions of business, law, public administration, and social work" (quoted in Matthews, 1977, p. 112). Deeds soon followed words, and the lights began to go out all over "pure" social science.

The second, larger LCRC grant, given in 1927, was a five-year grant and was not renewed. Ruml was made dean of the Division of the Social Sciences, which, by then, was in disarray. This situation was compounded by the university's new president, Robert Hutchins, who was highly skeptical of quantitative social science and who expressed personal hostility toward Ogburn. Merriam, himself disappointed in the failure of his vision of interdisciplinary research, turned to the task of building up professional public administration, which the Rockefeller sources supported generously both at Chicago and through the SSRC.

The same kind of Rockefeller arrangements, though considerably less munificent, established academic social science research at several other institutions: North Carolina, Columbia, Harvard, Stanford, Yale, Texas, and Virginia. This list includes several universities with departments that were later to become major sociology graduate programs, although only at North Carolina was sociology the main beneficiary of the funds. Howard Odum's Institute for Research in Social Science at North Carolina was the major center for sociological research in the South in the interwar period, the home of the journal *Social Forces*, and an important force for southern liberalism on the race question. Odum was enterprising, however, and he obtained a great deal of publicity through such projects as his collections of Negro work songs. He was also successful in gaining funds from other foundations. The Rockefeller Foundation expected the university to match its funds and ultimately to replace them, an improbability made into an impossibility by the Great Depression. The original five-year Rockefeller grant was renewed for three years in 1932, at reduced levels, and again until 1939-1940, at which point the annual sum was only $5,000 (Johnson and Johnson, 1980, p. 115), but this seems to have reflected the Foundation's desire to keep the university itself on the hook (for part of the negotiation process involved coercing the university into creating a School of Public Administration as a condition for renewal [Johnson and Johnson, 1980, p. 112]).

Odum nevertheless created a community of sociologists with some distinctive "subcultural" traits. The department was a bastion of correlational methods—a consequence of Odum's own Columbia biases, but also a result of the presence of T. J. Woofter, Jr., who was the author of the first multiple correlation dissertation in sociology at Columbia, in 1920. But Odum's orientation was regional, and the university was, relative to northern universities, impoverished. The department nevertheless successfully recruited talented students from the South, although many of them were attracted primarily by the idea of regional reform and were, therefore, oriented to specifically southern problems rather than sociology as a discipline.

Rural sociology was for the most part freed from dependence on foundations, although rural topics remained major concerns of foundations long after the Purnell Act of 1925 institutionalized government support for social research in the agricultural college/agricultural experiment station system. But the conditions were not ideal. The political character of the institutions encouraged a peculiar kind of community study, which often did little more than praise the character traits of the farmers in a region or the friendliness and church-going qualities of a community. This practice was justified, as Galpin put it in his autobiography, by the desire to combat "the general attitude of worsening farm life in the eyes of the public." A more legitimate motive behind this practice was rural morale, for "to cheapen farm life for any reason was to my mind very poor psychology in one seeking to improve farm life" (Galpin, 1938, p. 48). But politics constrained publication in other ways. The price that rural sociology had to pay for the largess of research support was the development of a strong internal sense of these political limits and a heavy bias toward quantification.[14] In time, the distinctive resource base led to the separation, always partial but always consequential, of rural sociology from the rest of the discipline. Organizational separation followed, and the Rural Sociological Society was established in 1935 and began to publish its own journal.[15]

The Social Science Research Counsel and the National Problem of Funding

The SSRC had a wide mandate, which involved a large tool kit of patronage devices and considerable funds. But virtually all of these funds derived from Rockefeller sources, with the result that the leadership was always anxious to act in terms of the expectations of their contacts at the Foundation. The aims of the SSRC changed over time, and, although it considered doing so, the SSRC never became a full-fledged research institute, like the ISRR, with a permanent staff. By the 1930s, the rationalization of governmental administration had become its major goal, and the creation of public administration as an academic field was one of the major consequences of its efforts in this period. But its initial aim was the transformation of the social sciences.

By the time of the emergence of the SSRC, the Rockefeller charities, like most of the other large foundations, had stopped making "no strings attached" block grants to universities. In response to this situation, Robert Merriam contrived to create a committee of the American Political Science Association (APSA) on "political research," which reported in 1922. In the ASS, a similar committee with the Orwellian title Committee on the Standardization of Research was revived in 1917 and headed by John Gillin (the original committee by this name had been created in 1912 as an analogue to a teaching committee that had the task of surveying teaching). These committees were the opening gambits in a political struggle that was to define the future of these disciplines, and in each case they were heralds of other organizational maneuvers that were enormously consequential for these young disciplines. Gillin's committee reported in 1920, as follows:

> What we need is the organization of those interested in research in sociology to map the field, discuss methods, work out a plan of cooperation and secure money to promote research. . . . We must also interest rich men in providing money for the prosecution of research until we have shown niggardly boards and legislatures the importance of finding out the facts bearing on questions of social theory and social policy. (quoted in Rhoades, 1981, pp. 13-14)

In 1922, the then-president of the ASS, James P. Lichtenberger, who had been a Columbia graduate student peer of Gillin's, presented a proposal to join Merriam in his efforts to organize the SSRC for precisely this purpose. Gillin and Stuart Chapin were appointed as the representatives of the ASS.[16]

In early 1923 a meeting was held by representatives of three societies, now including the American Economics Association (AEA), with the aim of creating for social science an analogue to the National Research Council, which then represented only the natural sciences. Stuart Chapin, Howard Odum, and John Gillin were prime movers in the new organization. The political purposes of the SSRC were complex and the stress on interdisciplinary work had many sources. Interdisciplinarity was part of the Rockefeller ideal of "realistic study," and it had its academic advocates as well. Merriam argued that the borrowing of methods was the best means of making political science "scientific" and that the use of such methods was nondisciplinary. Theory was, in contrast, disciplinary. Another source was the desire of the SSRC leadership to produce what their funding sources expected—social science research of practical value to policymakers. This aim was intensely felt by some participants in the SSRC, less by others. Throughout this period, members of the old school of reform surveying and of the reform foundation networks in

New York City, such as Shelby Harrison of the Russell Sage Foundation, were powerful figures in the SSRC who continued to press their meliorist views. This advocacy served as a continuous source of tension within the organization as well as in the relationship of the organization to its sponsors in the Rockefeller organizations.

There were, in the end, few tangible effects of this interdisciplinary thrust on the kinds of work the Council supported, but one effect was to create a new domain of tasks that was not subject to disciplinary criticism and demands for democracy within disciplinary organizations, such as ASS, AEA, and APSA. Another effect was to create a kind of central source of both authority and legitimacy—that is, SSRC—in the eyes of donors for social science as a whole. The means at the disposal of the SSRC for this purpose were large, but it was far from clear how they might be used. In 1927, three major Rockefeller grants were given: $750,000 for a general project fund to be spent over 5 years; $550,000 for administration over a 10-year period; and $500,000 for the development and publication of a *Journal of Social Science Abstracts*, which was proposed and subsequently edited by Stuart Chapin. An additional grant from Julian Rosenwald, Jr., instigated by Ruml, added $50,000 to the fund for administrative expenses. With this enormous base, the Council expanded its aims. In 1929, the high point of optimism, the Council adopted seven principle objectives: improvement of research organization; development of research personnel; enlargement, improvement, and preservation of research materials; improvement of research methods; dissemination of methods and results of investigation; facilitation of research work; and enhancement of the public appreciation of the significance of the social sciences. These aims ultimately changed.

The mode of funding adopted by the SSRC, which initially favored conferences (particularly a series of summer meetings at Dartmouth), presumed that the advocates of a "scientific" approach to social life needed only to discuss the central issues and come to agreements over how to transform research in the social sciences. The conferences organized by Merriam on "the new political science" in the 1920s were the fullest application of this strategy, but they turned into an intellectual fiasco. Topics that were the subject of disagreement prior to the meetings were generally left in a muddle after them. Yet the conferences had the effect of establishing and reestablishing personal relationships, and this "networking" was important for those sociologists who attended governing meetings as well as those on special topics. These large meetings were a victim of the reductions in funding of the 1930s and of their visible ineffectiveness.

The Depression altered the conflict between "pure" and "policy-relevant" social science in the decided favor of policy relevance. The projects undertaken during this period reflected the policy issues of the day, but their effects on sociology were not great. Many of the Columbians and beneficiaries of SSRC support contributed to Ogburn's compilation, *Recent Social Trends*, which made Ogburn a public figure and placed him on some of the boards that flourished in the Roosevelt administration. But the report itself, commissioned by President Hoover, was a dead letter when it arrived, since Franklin D. Roosevelt had just been elected. The sociologists, notably Odum, who worked closely with Ogburn to produce the report, complained bitterly about their exclusion from policy-making during the Depression. In the end, Ogburn ran into the same problems over factuality and objectivity that Wright and Oliver had 50 years earlier in the Massachusetts Bureau.[17] In fact, the model of policy science was as incoherent as it had been in 1875; Ogburn was simply not as politically adept as Colonel Wright had been.

The basic tool that the SSRC used to influence the social sciences was the selective provision of funds for activities that conformed with its goals. In the 1930s, when resources were limited, the main tool was fellowships for students. The Council financed a large number of postdoctoral research fellowships, of which 34 were awarded to sociologists, including Herbert Blumer, Samuel Stouffer, John Dollard, Charles Loomis, and Louis Wirth. A grants-in-aid program was created to enable scholars to complete writing projects, and conferences were held during the summer in Hanover, New Hampshire, to which the senior scholars in Council circles were invited. In the 1930s, when the main shared activity of the sociologists in the leadership positions of SSRC became the allocation of fellowships, a kind of "consensus" arose around evaluative preferences. What became a matter of importance beyond tradition departmental boundaries was the assessment of talent and the research directions in which this talent was being directed.

Given the initial institution of the networks that created the SSRC, it is no surprise that there was a heavy bias in the activities of the organization toward empirical and especially statistical research. Agitation for improvements in the mathematical training of social scientists became a continuing theme for the organization.[18] The Rockefeller representatives tended to prefer quantitative economic and business research, and in the "interdisciplinary" world of SSRC decision making, this meant that when proposals for the social sciences as a whole were produced, those which fit this model best were most likely to be supported. The substantive problems selected for examination by the Council, which created and funded the committees that sponsored the actual research, were typically on topics with a heavily quantitative content and some claim to policy relevance, such as the migration of rural blacks to northern cities.

ORGANIZATIONAL RESOURCES AND THE CHANGING STRUCTURE OF DISCIPLINARY POWER AND PRESTIGE

The case of Robert Lynd, the lead author of *Middletown*, provides a useful point of departure for assessing the organizational resources available to the sociologist of the day. The weakness of what Pitirim Sorokin later railed at as "the guild" of professional sociologists is made apparent by the ease with which Lynd became a "sociologist." Put crudely, one might say that Lynd was an intelligent and socially committed young man who rose through the foundation world of New York City to one of the best positions in academic sociology without ever having learned much sociology or taken any interest in the central intellectual issues of theory and method in the discipline.[19]

What made this possible? Part of the answer is that the leadership of the foundations had little respect for the internal academic hierarchy of sociology, and administrators and board members at Harvard and Columbia had even less. Within some very broad and vague limits, they could call whomever they liked a sociologist, and Lynd fell within these limits because *Middletown* was a book that was well received—though better received by the general public than by the profession.[20] More important, Lynd himself was socially acceptable and trustworthy, having proved himself as a worker in foundation circles for almost a decade.

At the moment of Lynd's ascent, the foundations and the circles in which Lynd was personally well known were at the height of their power. But this was to change almost immediately after his appointment, with the cutbacks of 1932. In general, the relation between sociology and reform had changed in the 1920s because many of the reform organizations had declined or been replaced by foundation-supported research agencies, such as the ISRR and the various municipal bureaus. The professionalization and bureaucratization of social work meant the end or transformation of the charity societies.[21] With the Depression, the financial resources of the reform movements and their successors ceased to be important for sociology. The reform impulse did not disappear, of course, but the intellectualizations of the impulse increasingly took the form of therapeutic ideologies or were linked to professional or bureaucratic interests.

The 1930s saw the transformation of the ASS from an organization whose members were primarily interested in reform topics to one whose members were academics. At the beginning of the Depression, all membership organizations were hard hit; those members who were merely interested citizens dropped their subscriptions, and total membership dropped, at least in the worst years of the Depression. But patterns differed, even within the social sciences. The APSA continued to grow: in 1930, its total membership was 1800; almost a decade later, it was 2800; and in

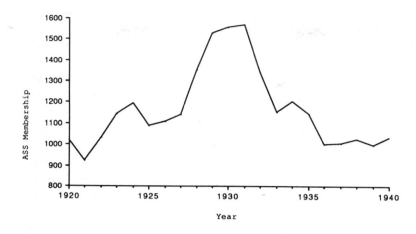

Figure 2.1. ASS Membership 1920 to 1940

1945 it was 3300 (Somit and Tanenhaus, 1982, pp. 91-92). As Figure 2.1 documents, the ASS lost ground, dropping from a high of nearly 1600 in 1930-1931 to a stable level of around 1000 by the end of the 1930s.

Who were the members who remained? During the early 1930s there were estimates that the number of members in doctorate-granting departments were only around 130. By 1950, when membership in the "activity" category was back up to 1634, some 1168 held "liberal arts" academic appointments and another 117 held appointments in professional schools. Thus 79% were in higher education (Riley, 1960, p. 922). The membership by this period did not comprise a very high proportion of the persons identifying themselves as sociologists, however. In 1940, the proportion of members of the Southern Sociological Society who were also members of the ASS was only 28.3%, a figure that did not increase significantly until the 1980s (Simpson, 1988, p. 63).

The ASS was very far from being a democratic institution. Nevertheless, in contrast to the SSRC, which was far less responsive to the interests and needs of ordinary academics, it was relatively open. The presidency was voted on by the membership as a whole, and established sociologists could not be easily excluded from political participation. In the 1930s, this organization became, for the first time, the scene of major political struggles.[22] No clear line of succession exists between the various events that went into the creation of a divided discipline in the 1930s, and nothing so simple as a dispute explains the course of events. The most famous event involved the dissolution of the society's formal relationship to the *American Journal of Sociology* (*AJS*) and the subsequent establishment of the *American Sociological Review* (*ASR*) as the society's official journal. But the dispute over the *AJS* was not in any simple sense a revolt against the dominance of the University of Chicago, for the critics of the journal included Chicago graduates of an earlier generation. Moreover, the "Chicago" sociologists who dominated the journal were representatives of no special "school." What they did represent, as the critics of the journal tirelessly stressed, was a new arrogance, based on access to funding and embodied in what was seen as the misuse of power over participation in ASS programs and publication in the journal (Bannister, 1987; Meroney, 1931).

Dissatisfaction and the need to seek new organizational venues and to exercise new kinds of organizational power were felt on each side of the increasingly fragmented discipline. The usual difficulties of voluntary organizations in making decisions through committees and votes consumed a great deal of energy and contributed to feelings of ill will. As a consequence, the benign rivalries that had replaced the personal bitterness of the founding generation during the 1920s became equally bitter conflicts within the society itself and between the society and the discipline. One manifestation of this was the rapid expansion of new journals and organizations. *Rural Sociology* was founded in 1936, in part as a consequence of the dispute over *AJS*. The secession of the Rural Sociology Section from the ASS followed in 1938, and the new Rural Sociological Society began with 206 members.

Other specialty organizations with boundaries overlapping those of the ASS followed. For example, during this period the

National Council on Family Relations and the American Catholic Sociological Society was created, and the major regional associations began to emerge. The Southern Sociological Society (the largest of the regional associations) was established in 1936, the Midwest in 1936, the Southwestern in 1937, the Ohio Valley in 1938 (Simpson, 1988, p. 8), and the Pacific Sociological Association in 1930-1931. The Sociological Research Association (SRA), an elite invitation-only factional group that limited its membership to 100 internally elected members, was established in the same period.[23] One might consider these foundings to be signs of disciplinary vitality, but the contrast with the increasing membership of the APSA during this period suggests something different. Sociology was becoming a considerably more fragmented discipline, and the ASS in the 1930s was not successful at encompassing its various interests.

The case of the SRA, which had no parallels in political science or other nearby disciplines, is especially revealing in this connection. The organization represented an attempt to define and create an elite through co-optation, a strategy that was chosen only because the fragmentation of the discipline rendered the ASS uncontrollable and the academic hierarchy of the discipline was incapable of perpetuating itself within ASS. As a sign of the declining dominance of elite universities, the percentage of Ph.D. theses produced by Columbia and Chicago decreased throughout the 1920s, from a peak of 72% of the total Ph.D.'s in American sociology in 1918 to 32.8% in 1928. Furthermore, the reputational rankings of departments published in 1925 and 1934 told a reasonably consistent story: in 1925, Chicago, Columbia, and Minnesota outstripped the competition, with Wisconsin a little distance back; in 1934, the five departments rated "most distinguished" (in no special order) were Columbia, Chicago, Minnesota, North Carolina, and Wisconsin. But these rankings had little significance as an index of the power of departments to place their graduates in other top departments. For example, a disproportionate number of appointments at Chicago were Chicago Ph.D.'s and, in general, the "top" departments did not consistently hire from one another. Rising departments such as Harvard managed to elevate themselves without hiring graduates from the top departments. By the 1930s, the only department that could boast of having placed graduates in each of the other major five departments were Columbia in the Giddings era; Robert MacIver and Robert Lynd were unable to duplicate the feat. Thus no continuous interchange of students was established, and the "elite" departments did not have placement records that were very much different from nonelite departments.

Yet as a teaching enterprise, both at the graduate and undergraduate levels, sociology preserved and expanded its resource base. The expansion of sociology into undergraduate institutions and the demand for Ph.D.-holding faculty in these institutions were the growth sectors of the 1930s. This expansion enabled increases in the numbers of new Ph.D.'s to continue through the next decade, as illustrated in Figure 2.2. The increases were unexpected. Indeed, in 1934 Ellsworth Faris and Stuart Chapin had an exchange over what was assumed to be the inevitable oversupply of Ph.D.'s, with Faris arguing that the oversupply would have to be absorbed by government employment (Chapin, 1934; Faris, 1934).[24]

The effect of growth in a situation where the new departments, such as Harvard and Duke, did not share in a strong consensus over the appropriate training for sociologists caused further fragmentation of sociology. Indeed, these new departments trained students in new ways and had conceptions of the discipline that differed from the reigning conceptions at Chicago and Columbia.

Yet another sign of fragmentation in the 1930s revolved around differences between "college" and "university" sociology, reflected in the contents of textbooks and the careers of the leading textbook authors. The textbooks of the day and the writings directed at a wider public had a great deal in common. This fact was probably critical to the expansion of sociology to the smaller colleges, many of which were denominational. A writer such as Charles Ellwood, whose works on social reconstruction were directed to literate churchgoers and ministers, legitimated the discipline as a part of a rounded Christian education, and a writer like Harry Elmer Barnes made an acquaint-

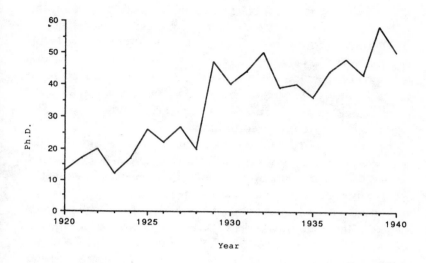

Figure 2.2. Sociology Ph.D.'s 1920 to 1940

ance with sociology appear to be a necessary element of the citizenship and the social conscience that women's colleges sought to cultivate. The teachers in these colleges did not share the values or interests of the members of the SRA, and, much like today, they did not depend on the latter's writings, much less their scientific authority. Rather, they depended on the textbook literature, and on their ability to attract students. In a sense, these older textbooks are the material remains of the interactions between teachers and students, and their content and style is revealing. For example, a work like Barnes's very successful social problems text for Prentice-Hall (1942) demanded a great deal more in the way of cultural literacy than present texts do and contained messages aimed directly at the prejudices from which students were then emancipating themselves. Intellectual emancipation took the form of demonstrating the premise that the arrangements under which social problems were handled reflect interest-politics and irrational dogmas. Many of the textbooks of the day were distinguished works by important sociologists, and they spoke directly to the beliefs of their audience and attempted to transform them. In this respect, then, these books carried on the Wardian aim of edification at the very time it was being expunged from the more "advanced" graduate programs. But their message made sociology effective as an undergraduate course of study. As a result, the number of texts for every substantive field in sociology far outstripped rates of increase in any other aspect of American sociology.[25]

Had the more elite sociologists, funded by the foundations, scored any unambiguous cognitive successes that were relevant across the various domains of sociology, the fragmentation of the 1930s might not have occurred. At the very least, the discipline might have been restructured in a way that reduced its dependence on the intellectually less successful parts of the discipline. But there were no such successes; the founding of the SRA represented an effort to sustain a common methodological ground among the field's dominant figures and, at the same time, to co-opt the well-connected and talented younger sociologists. But this common ground was not shared with the discipline at large, creating a rift that persists to the present day.

The ASS, its rivals, and the new journals were each organizational resources. They were means by which sociologists could make their voices heard to an interested audience, legitimate their work to their academic employers, and deal with the problems of maintaining their resource base. Each of the new organizations represented a different constituency or combination of constituencies. But the distribution of organizational resources and the diversity of resource bases evident by the end of the 1930s, coupled with the inability of the ASS to expand at the same rate as the discipline, meant something of great significance: the various kinds of sociology that could be practiced in the American setting could easily find a means of sustaining themselves and could, therefore, ignore the others. Some of the enterprises were virtually autonomous. For example, rural sociology soon had academic departments that produced Ph.D.'s and effectively left the discipline. But other points of division were complex, as is evident in the relation between the liberal arts colleges and the research universities with graduate programs. The universities relied on the colleges to produce prospective Ph.D. students, although sociology graduate students were often recruited from other sources, such as adjacent departments and the ministry. In turn, the colleges relied on the universities to train their teachers. But the links were not very constraining, nor as strong as the internal demands of each university and college.

EFFORTS AT SYMBOLIC UNIFICATION: METHODS IN THE INTERWAR YEARS

The Methodological Dispute of the 1930s

The network of persons involved in the SSRC had privileged access to foundation support and a strong sense of a shared superiority to the mass of the discipline. By the end of the 1930s that source of superiority was not very meaningful, for there were few foundation funds being given to sociology. Yet this group was "the establishment," and the criticisms of this establishment and its internal controversies were the source for some of the most interesting writing of the period. The controversy over method of the 1930s began with Charles Ellwood's *Methods in Sociology* (1933), an attack on the methodological views of the SSRC establishment, and closed with Lynd's *Knowledge for What?* ([1939] 1967), an insider's attempt to influence the course and conception of foundation-funded social research. Both attempts failed. More generally, the longer political history of the SSRC's attempts to make social science "scientific" was itself a history of failure, especially if we look only at the extent to which social scientists were persuaded to adopt a consensual viewpoint on the nature of science.[26] In the 1920s, for instance, there emerged a kind of aggressive empiricism that took as its object the de-legitimation of "theory" and the "philosophical method," actively seeking their exclusion from the discipline and especially from graduate education.[27] In the absence of a coherent methodological doctrine to debate, however, discussions degenerated into slogan making and baiting.

The topic produced an extraordinary amount of heat, in part because of the strong negative reaction of many sociologists to the funding decisions and selective biases of the SSRC. The criticisms by Sorokin of Ogburn's *Recent Social Trends* (President's Committee on Social Trends), for example, were brutal (Bannister, 1987, pp. 185-187). Although it was not an SSRC product, Ogburn's work was the best expression of several elements of the SSRC idea and came closest to the aims of the Rockefeller supporters of the SSRC, and so the critics took its shortcomings as representative of what Charles Beard called "the coming crisis in the empirical method to which American social science had been so long in bondage" (quoted in Bannister, 1987, p. 186).

Ellwood's critique (1933), the most comprehensive attack on what he could construct as the SSRC conception, is instructive as a guide to the premises of the new elite and the differences between the parties to the dispute. Ogburn is the paradigmatic figure for Ellwood's critique, and it is Ogburn and Rice who are the object of the bulk of his criticisms. The main conflict, Ellwood argued, is between those who defend a narrow view of the aims and methods of sociology, based on the philosophy of science of Mach and Pearson, and those like himself who are methodological pluralists and accept a role for synthetic reason and criticism in sociology. Many other disputes over the boundaries of sociology could be seen to align with this main contrast. For example, the dispute over appropriate audiences for sociology, over its social mission, over the role and epistemic character of evaluative discourse, over the boundaries between this evaluative discourse and scientific discourse, over the nature of hypotheses and their relation to conceptual thinking, over the relative importance of traditional scholarly "learning" to the mastery of "techniques," over the kind of data to be preferred (and especially the scientific admissibility of historical documents and the results of participant observation and sympathetic introspection), over the status of proper causal explanation as contrasted to correlation, and, most important, over the question of the reducibility of the subjective and cultural realms to measurement.[28] All these disputes, Ellwood argued, are traceable to the question of theory, method, and the role of criticism in the field.

Ellwood's characterization of the situation—that sociology was "divided into hostile schools which mutually seek to undermine and discredit one another" (1933, p. 3)—was amply justified by the response to his book. Although it received many favorable reviews, and although the seriousness and legitimacy of its arguments were demonstrated in subsequent years, the book was ridiculed by one of the older members of the new elite, Ellsworth Faris, in an *AJS* review that provided a timely confirmation of the charges of arrogance being leveled against this elite in the ASS. Faris's reply was a purely sloganistic defense of the claim that the natural science method was appropriate to the social sciences:

> The author would like to contrast social science with natural science. But that is just the issue, for social life is also natural. . . . All is natural. Murder is natural, and suicide, theft, divorce, and race prejudice. Capone is as much a product of nature as Lindbergh. (1934b, p. 688)

In the face of this kind of response, serious discussion of the issues could not proceed, and methodological debate itself became discredited. For the generation of Stouffer and Lazarsfeld it was taboo, but elements of the dispute with Ellwood continued among the insiders.

From the mid-1930s on, there were two further debates within SSRC circles: (1) the debate between the "scientific" social scientists and the remaining reformers, such as Shelby Harrison and Robert Lynd; and (2) the emerging debate over the quantification of the subjective, in which Herbert Blumer and Samuel Stouffer figure prominently. Blumer's (1939) views can be found in his critique of *The Polish Peasant* (Thomas and Znaniecki, 1918), presented at a special SSRC conference on methods. This critique was short on originality, and in part it repeated the essentialist arguments on the nature of human action given by Ellwood,

who had been Blumer's teacher the decade before. Lynd's arguments are more interesting, especially as an expression of the
mentality of the foundation-oriented New York reformers on the
eve of what was to be a huge expansion of support for the social
sciences.

Lynd's analysis reflected the SSRC experience and adheres
closely to the original antidisciplinary premises of the Rockefeller
leadership, suggesting that sociology give up its synthetic pretensions and become problem oriented. But he argues that the
move toward quantification, although "essentially healthy," has
had deleterious effects because the refinements of methods have
been applied to traditional disciplinary problems ([1939] 1967,
p. 17) and served the aims of career advancement within disciplinary specializations (p. 18). What is needed, he argues, is a
renewed assault on the problems of mankind, understood as
"cultural" problems, or more precisely problems requiring the
reform of culture with the aim of better meeting human needs.
The focus of this work, he believes, ought to be in culture and
personality studies (p. 52), by which he means the kind of work
done by his old ISRR ally Lawrence Frank (p. 71). The problem
with disciplinary social science is that it fails to go beyond amel-
ioration that "asks no questions that fundamentally call into
question or go substantially beyond the core of the folkways"
(p. 144). The object of social science should be to reform the
folkways, for as Lynd tells us, "whenever our current culture is
found to cramp or distort the quest of considerable numbers of
persons for the satisfaction of basic cravings of human personality, there lies a responsibility for social science" (p. 205). To dis-
charge this responsibility in action would inevitably require "a
large and pervasive extension of planning and control to many
areas now left to casual individual initiative" (p. 209). Against
those (like Ellwood) with an outdated faith in education for
democratic action (p. 236), we must accept that

> the chance of securing more coherent, constructive behavior
> from persons depends upon recognizing the large degree of
> irrationality that is natural to them and upon structuring

the culture actively to support and encourage intelligent types of behavior, including inevitably opportunity for creative spontaneous expression of emotion. (p. 234)

It will suffice to say that some form of this idea was behind the investment of the foundations in "social psychology" in the postwar period, as well as in the Carnegie Corporation's financing and direction of the American Dilemma project, topics to be considered in the next chapter.

The Triumph of Attitude Measures and the New Survey Methods

By the time Ellwood's book (1933) was published, the social psychological literature had developed in such a way that his claims about the inadequacy of quantitative methods in the face of the subjective realm were decreasingly relevant. The practice of attitude measurement was advancing rapidly, and the literature was expanding enormously. Indeed, the social psychological portion of sociology was taking center stage on the strength of the problem of attitude. The key developments were the use of survey techniques borrowed from advertising research and the rise of Samuel Stouffer and Paul Lazarsfeld. Stouffer was the ultimate SSRC insider. He and Frederic Stephan, among a number of others who were primarily demographers, continued the Chicago developments in quantification, though these now turned in the new and transformative direction of sampling and measurement. The transformation was in part a matter of funding. A few projects continued to be funded by the foundations, such as the radio research performed by Lazarsfeld. The techniques and intellectual inspiration for this work derived from sources outside of sociology, notably pollsters and commercial market researchers who had a much more elaborate funding base to perform large-scale questionnaire surveys. Sampling theory, a technical development that was just being made available in the late 1930s, put survey work of this sort within the grasp of academic researchers.

The work done by Stouffer and Lazarsfeld stood on its own resource base. It was, therefore, unnecessary to legitimate it as "sociology" in order to get it funded, and, consequently, they were free to avoid the methodological disputes of the time. Stouffer's writings of the 1930s were careful to avoid them. In fact, he not only did not reject alternative "methods," such as the case study and the historical method, he suggested that they serve purposes beyond "the vision of a mathematical regression with its range of chance error known." Moreover, "as the goal of one's research," he argued, this vision "may help thinking out one's problem, but often is not a very useful conception to follow out to its literal end," because

> the constants in the population of possibilities underlying a good many of our problems are probably shifting too fast in time or varying too much from place to place to justify spending money on the intricate kind of study which can be made profitably in physics or even biology. And, too often, numerical indexes of crucial factors are of unknown reliability or nonexistent. (1934, p. 485)

This kind of argument ignored the ultimate methodological goals of their predecessors and the disputes that concern about these goals had caused:

> In the case of juvenile delinquency, for example, it is hard to conceive of a mathematical equation, however compli- cated, which will be of much value unaccompanied by juvenile delinquency data of a nonquantitative nature, in- cluding, perhaps, documents whose interpretation is essen- tially an artistic procedure. And why, indeed, should we care whether or not our methods are copies of those used in the more nearly exact fields of natural science? *The Jack Roller* may more nearly resemble art than science, as the word *science* is conventionally used by scientists, but if the

study helps us to understand delinquency for a few years, it ought to be good sociology. Why not, one ventures to suggest, declare a moratorium on the use of the word *science* as applied to studies of social phenomena? To *limit* ourselves to measurement would sterilize research. (Stouffer, 1934, p. 486)

These passages convey a series of messages: the refusal to join in discussions of the "scientific" character of sociology and the acceptance of a pregiven standard of "good sociology" that does not rest on such conceptions. This pragmatic approach was attractive to foundation leaders, with whom Stouffer developed excellent relationships, and it was attractive to graduate students. But it served to disconnect "empirical sociology" from the large but uncomfortable questions that were raised in the tradition of theory.

FAILURES TO SYMBOLICALLY UNIFY: THEORY IN THE INTERWAR PERIOD

In the late 1920s and 1930s, "theory" meant what it had meant before the war: the history of social thought and conceptions of progressive change. Floyd House (1936), Charles Ellwood (1938), and Harry Elmer Barnes and Howard Becker (1938) published important historical surveys; Pitirim Sorokin published his multivolume *Social and Cultural Dynamics* (1937); and Chapin wrote on cultural change. The most ambitious "theoretical" text of the early 1930s, E. E. Eubank's *The Concepts of Sociology: A Treatise Presenting a Suggested Organization of Sociological Theory in Terms of its Major Concepts* (1932), gives a good indication of the receptive atmosphere for Talcott Parsons's *The Structure of Social Action* (1937) as well as a baseline against which the influence of this and Parsons's later works, such as *The Social System* (1951) and *Toward a General Theory of Action* (Parsons and Shils, 1951), may be judged.

Eubank was a student of Small and opened his book with an excerpt of an encouraging letter from Small, dated in 1926 shortly before the latter's death. Small wrote that there was a "peculiar timelessness" to Eubank's effort. The sociological revolt, of which Small himself had been a part, was

> essentially a protest against the ideas which dominated the social sciences that the human lot is some sort of glacial gravitation of particles without other connection than aggregation in masses. The sociologists pinned their faith to an insight that in some way or other human destinies are intimately related with one another. This was the secret of their attempt to find the secret of life by following out the analogy between "the social organism" and the animal organism. That proved to be a false clue, but it led to the psychological nexus which we are trying to interpret. Meanwhile the sociologists are specializing so minutely upon particular types of human groupings that they are in danger of losing sight of human society as a whole. (quoted in Eubank, 1932, p. ix)

Eubank's problem was to come up with a kind of systematization of sociology's key concepts with the hope of finding a substitute for the unity promised by Spencerian sociology and the organic analogy. But this task had to be performed in the face of what now was a quite startling diversity of concepts, each of which had established itself in connection with research or in the textbook literature by the end of the 1920s.

Eubank's analytical list of concepts is too long to be reproduced here. Suffice it to say that it includes many of the same elements later included in Parsons's scheme, under slightly different names and with somewhat different points of emphasis. Moreover, it also includes many ideas derived from evolutionism, particularly the variety that laid stress on the competitive relations between groups and the dependence of folkways on the material and political realities of human existence. Eubank comes to the conclusion that "by restating our major points in terms of *action* a basis of synthesis of the entire body of material becomes at once apparent" (1932, p. 386).[29] His remarks on the "conceptual disarray" of contemporary sociology are worth quoting, for they read as a prologue to the Parsonian era.

> [However] natural and explicable this condition may have been in the past, its continuance constitutes a serious handicap both to sociological teaching and to research, to say nothing of the way in which the discipline itself is left vulnerable thereby to the attacks of its none too sympathetic critics. (p. 50)

These opinions were widely shared, as Eubank shows by quotations from peers as diverse as Robert MacIver, Read Bain, Hornell Hart, George Lundberg, Pitirim Sorokin, Floyd House, and one of the Europeans known to American audiences as a systematic "theorist," Leopold von Wiese. In particular, there was a strong sense that psychology and economics had their conceptual houses in order and that sociology suffered by comparison (p. 48). Evidently this was widely shared, for Eubank's work became one of the most widely cited texts of the era.

Parsons's immediate sources were different than Eubank's. Parsons built on a variant of the organic analogy that was locally fashionable in the 1930s at Harvard as a consequence of the influence of the activist scientists, L. J. Henderson and W. D. Cannon. In a sense, Parsons simply returned to the mode that the earlier sociologists had found inadequate, the teleological mode of explanation and organicism, while abandoning all the complex concepts that had been proposed as substitutes, such as "social process," "social control," "group conflict," and the like. These were jettisoned for reasons of conceptual economy and theoretical coherence.[30]

The way this coherence was to be achieved had a great deal to do with Parsons's situation at Harvard and his personal need to establish sociology as a science with a distinctive and autonomous theoretical problem. The problem he identifies in *The Structure of Social Action* (1937)—that is, the "Hobbesian" problem of order—was not original, even in American sociology. Giddings too had held that "the most important question in sociology . . . was to explain the fact of society," [31] but Parsons managed to convey to many of the Harvard graduate students of the 1930s that this was a problem for which there were theoretical answers and that devotion to its resolution could constitute a satisfactory intellectual life.

The Parsonian project, with its plethora of subtasks of conceptual refinement within the larger system, was thus a viable form of academic practice, which met a set of student needs quite distinct from the needs met by Chicago sociology or the traditional conversion from reform sentimentalism.[32] Parsons was the first teacher of graduate students since Small himself to convert sociology students into theorists in significant numbers. Indeed, the Harvard department prided itself at this time on the visibility of its theorists and the departmental stress on theory, which Sorokin in particular had been able to make attractive to Harvard undergraduates. There was no realistic hope of making this topic into a pure discipline that would be widely studied in small colleges or which would attract large numbers of state university students. Parsons himself had no such illusions, and his own work developed in a way that reconciled his vision of sociology as a profession to some of these realities of demand.

CONCLUSION

The interwar years set the stage for much that was to make American sociology unique. Slowly, sociology penetrated the curriculum of colleges and universities, but this occurred without any widely accepted standardization of theory and method. Despite this failure of standardization, methodology became increasingly quantitative, initially under the granting system established by the Rockefeller foundations. Yet even as surveys and quantitative analysis prospered before the war, especially in the measurement of "attitudes," there was considerable disagreement over how to conduct research. In the arena of theory, there were very few coherent paradigms to integrate the diverse research findings of the many empirical studies being done with surveys, and other methods as well. In the wake of the collapse of organicism and evolutionism was an emerging social psychology that focused on action, but this focus could hardly be considered a unifying theory. There were still some of the older grand theories—Pitirim Sorokin's work could be seen as the exemplar—but most conceptualization was narrow, examining specific topics such as urban growth, ethnic relations, delinquency, cultural lags, and the like.

This lack of symbolic unity over methods and theory was reflected in the growing fragmentation of sociology's organizational base. As ASS membership declined in the 1930s, other sociology organizations began to proliferate, thereby fractioning the membership in different organizations. Moreover, the control of Columbia and Chicago over the discipline was weakening. And, as founding of the SRA underscored, a growing rift between elites and nonelites was emerging.

To an extent, these problems were to be suspended during the Second World War and its immediate aftermath. But they persisted, even during sociology's "Golden Era" in the 1960s and early 1970s. And, as the 1990s begin, the problems of securing material support, achieving consensus over theory and method, and consolidating organizational resources are as evident as they were in the late 1930s. Such is the story of the next two chapters.

NOTES

1. The larger study was the *Titanic* of the social survey movement, but troubles in the movement, mostly taking the form of pointless fact gathering that had no particular audience, were evident earlier. E. C. Lindeman, discussing the unusability of many of the surveys and the fact that they were a great disappointment from the point of view of "reform," observed in 1924 that the mania for surveys had produced many absurdities, such as the "rural county in the South [that] had been surveyed on seven different occasions and by seven different agencies" (1924, p. 6n).

2. Much of it was data of high quality, collected by experienced and academically competent persons, including Giddings's student Warren H. Wilson, who had begun survey work for the Presbyterian Board of Home Missions in 1912,

and many professors of sociology at state universities, who had been released from their institutions to perform the work. The survey method itself, then, began the transition from amateur to professional data collection.

3. The method of funding internally was through selecting "proposals," which were generated internally, approved in principle by the board of directors (which included a Rockefeller representative), and then worked on by the staff. The senior technical staff of about six persons usually worked in collaboration with the proponent to develop "objectives, methodology, extent and nature of the representative sample, the field procedure, time schedule and budget." Many times the proponent of the idea was made project director; the senior staff always kept the projects under close scrutiny, even through the final editing (Fisher, 1934, pp. 20-21).

4. Giddings, who was a pronounced cynic about the meliorative powers and aims of foundations, contributed to this process of definition in his "Forward" to Luther Fry's 1924 Columbia dissertation, done at the ISRR, *Diagnosing The Rural Church: A Study in Method*. As Giddings notes: "As a true scientific mind always does, [Fry] limits himself to a determination of fact and to the correlation (in the statistician's meaning of the word) of fact with fact, leaving to readers who may consult his work all questions of approval or disapproval of the conditions which his study reveals. He gives us diagnosis only" (Giddings, 1924a, p. v). This was not a formula that was always followed, but it was a means of formally reconciling meliorative aims imposed from outside with "research."

5. Throughout this period it is difficult to know what the terms mean in such expressions as "the tested methods and principles of social science," which is included in the statement of aims of the ISRR. In the case of Ruml, who later served as a dean at Chicago and who presumably was a sophisticate, there is evidence that these were little more than slogans. Mortimer Adler describes teaching a course with him at Chicago in which Ruml sat "Buddha-like" while Adler, an Aristotelian, lectured his faculty on logic and the true nature of science (1977, pp. 151-152). Similar questions arise in the later case of Frederick Osborne, a millionaire enthusiast for eugenics who transferred this enthusiasm to behavioral science and who was on the SSRC board from 1938 to 1953 and later was given a commission as a general during the Second World War. In this latter capacity he served as the superior to Samuel Stouffer. In each of these cases, as with Lynd, the support of these patronage intermediaries depended on their personal assessments of the ideas they dealt with, not an uncharacteristic feature of patronage systems.

6. The rationale given for this form of analysis was essentially the Pearsonian philosophy of science formulated by Giddings: "social laws cannot attain the same certainty as physical laws . . . because of the multiplicity of the stimuli that can operate in a given situation. . . . The effect of this fundamental fact is to exclude the possibility of arriving at social laws in the hard and categorical definition of that word" ([1924] 1974, p. 33). The study was professedly Pearsonian in method and intent. It also adhered to Giddings's ideas about measurement. The real aims of churches are, of course, spiritual and are therefore unmeasurable directly. The ISRR was interested in "psychological factors" and attitudes, and several studies measured them, including one done with Columbia Teacher's College which attempted to measure "traits such as deceit, self-

control, and cooperativeness" (Fisher, 1934, p. 15). The term *attitude* figures in the statements of the religious faction in the ISRR (cf. R. W. Fox, 1983, p. 113), but Fry declined to attempt to measure "Christian attitudes," brotherhood, and so on directly. He suggests "they can be measured indirectly" through such tangible facts as church attendance, contributions relative to means, and the like. These "measures" are the subject of his correlational efforts (Fry, 1924).

7. The terminus of the correlational methodology, reached in 1930, had been "a refined technique for evaluating the church in terms both of internal trends [*trends* is used here in Fry's technical sense, meaning a causal correlation, and as a substitute for the term *law*] and of the effects upon it of external forces" (Fisher, 1934, p. 18). The unit of analysis for these studies was the community or community institutions such as the church, not the idea per se. The reasons for this were both practical and technical. The computational requirements of correlational studies, especially those involving a great deal of partialling, such as the American Village studies, were prohibitive for surveys of individuals. Like Yule's reanalysis of Booth's outdoor relief data in 1899, the strategy was to use "ecological" correlations or measure properties of the institutions themselves (Yule, 1899). The 140 villages analyzed in *American Agricultural Villages* (Brunner, Hughes, and Patten, 1927) could thus be subject to elaborate, albeit very time-consuming and therefore expensive, correlational analysis, including a good deal of partialling. In contrast, a survey with 6000 responses could not have been subject to such analysis.

8. The best historical account of these struggles, based on the Lynd and ISRR papers, is that of Richard W. Fox (1983), which, however, is not reliable in its contextual remarks on the intellectual history either of social theory or social research. It grossly overstates Lynd's intellectual originality. Two points need to be kept in mind in discussing Lynd's rise: (1) the intellectual environment of New York Presbyterianism was heavily sociological in its orientation already and had long experience with sociologists and community religious study, especially in the Presbyterian Board of Home Missions, which gave Lynd his first preaching assignment; and (2) the organizational and personal networks of sociologists and liberal theologians and clerical reformers overlapped extensively, being largely friendly and mutually tolerant. What follows will rely more heavily on Helen Lynd's oral reminiscences (HML).

9. Some studies of the ISRR were delegated to university researchers. Park's studies of the problems of Orientals on the Pacific Coast had been partially funded by the ISRR, but the relationship had withered by 1925, when Park refused to accept the "editing" of the ISRR staff with respect to his claim that the Oriental Exclusion Act of 1924 had reduced tensions—a claim that the New York liberals of the ISRR could not regard as consistent with the meliorative educational aims of their research (Matthews, 1977, p. 114; cf. Lyman, 1972, on the theoretical premises of the analysis).

10. Merriam had contact with Giddings and took his course on the principles of sociology, but he was primarily a student of the political theorist W. A. Dunning.

11. The *Proceedings of the Academy of Political Science* of 1912 devoted a number to "Organization for Social Work," including several pieces by prominent representatives of the reform organizations of the day. These stressed the

importance of government statistics, the survey method, and the need for regulation not only of rapacious employers, exploiters of child labor, tenement owners, and the like, but also of such things as "public amusements." A sense of the mentality of the reformers on this subject may be gained by considering the article on amusements. The author of the article on this topic, Mrs. Belle Lindner Israels, Chairman of the Committee on Amusement Resources of Working Girls, explains that "In the city of Wilkes-Barre, Pennsylvania, where they have a population of about 65,000, between five and six thousand people nightly are visiting amusement places of all kinds, dance-halls, motion picture shows, vaudeville theatres and the like." There and elsewhere we "find the same standards, the same resources, affording the same resulting dangers, the same class of people making use of these places" (Israels, 1912, p. 123). The only solution to this "problem" is regulation, preferably by statute, licensing, and the creation of an office of public inspector. The moral and political basis for this peculiar juxtaposition of municipal socialism and killjoyism is the idea of collective obligation to provide for the need for recreation. "But we must also keep a watchful eye upon what is offered to the public commercially in the guise of amusement" (p. 126). At the time Park's training program was at its peak, a great deal of academic sociology still had this tone—though a somewhat different but parallel transformation was taking place in other parts of the discipline.

12. The term is Matthews's, who also quotes Park's various sayings on the subject of meliorism: " 'I do not belong to the evangelical school of sociology,' he remarked to an acquaintance, and his answer to a student's question, 'What did he do for people?' was a gruff 'Not a damn thing!' " (1977, p. 116). The personal transformation that students went through was not entirely unlike that described by such Columbia students as Gillin two decades before, but it was a transformation in a different direction, at once more intense and less intellectualized. Giddings was an arch rationalist who mocked theologians, and this was often attractive to the students of the theologians themselves. His students, notably Chapin and Ogburn, created a kind of cult of objectivity, an attitude toward "bias" that identified it, highly negatively, with "emotion" (Chapin, 1920, p. 4), which was contrasted to the state in which "the personal equation" (a phrase from astronomy denoting the distinctive systematic errors of observers recording positions of the stars) was "minimized" (p. 14). This was a formula that justified the use of instruments of measurement (like well-prepared interview schedules) and the aspiration to universality through replicability (pp. 14, 4). Park and especially Thomas shared the intellectual background to this attitude. In 1912, when Park was still working for Booker T. Washington, Thomas wrote to Park to suggest that they should "go to New York together and have some talk with any men you want to see and some I would like you to know better, such as Dewey and Robinson" (quoted in Raushenbush, 1979, p. 70). Robinson was the historian who was the embodiment of the Columbia spirit of debunking rationalism, exerting great influence on such sociologists as Harry Elmer Barnes, who in the interdisciplinary fashion of Columbia, became a historian as well. There was a marked difference between Park and Robinson. Park mocked the manners and sensibility of the middle-class students who came to him and gave them an ethos and sensibility in exchange; Robinson and his peers were specifically antireligious and concerned with what they regarded,

as Giddings (1928) put it in his own final testament, as "superstitious" reverence for received ideas. But, though they may have had contempt for its exponents (as Giddings did for the social worker E. T. Devine, whom he was nevertheless instrumental in advancing), they did not mock the reform sensibility as such, and several of Robinson's students in sociology, such as Gillin, Odum, Gehlke, Chapin, and Shenton, retained a strong sense of social mission. They resolved the problem of affectivity through the statistical approach itself and through the idea that testing against the numbers was the best guard against bias. This enabled them to see the possibility of normative conclusions as a result of sociological research and to consider this step as a part of "sociology" itself.

13. One student, Pauline Young, recalled an experience with Park that captures something of the kind of professional socialization he enforced with respect to "theory":

> Once as a graduate student I had rushed into print with an article on occupational attitudes of a sectarian group of laborers. I proudly sent a copy of this article to Dr. Park hoping to please him with my "conceptual thinking." His reply put ashes in my mouth. "You have ruined meticulously gathered data by couching them in concepts that sound like the grips and passes of a secret society." (quoted in Raushenbush, 1979, p. 184)

This did not mean that Park rejected abstractions or conceptual thinking; she learned that a concept is "in reality a definition of a social situation in shorthand" (quoted in Raushenbush, p. 184).

14. Galpin gave the example of a study conducted during his tenure in Washington as director of a unit of Farm Life Studies in the Department of Agriculture. The research was done on a cooperative basis with a state university by Carl C. Taylor, Carle Zimmerman, and Dale Yoder. The study dealt with a large rural community, entirely white, with a land-tenure and labor situation of stark inequality between landowners and the poor tenants and hired men. When the dean of the university's School of Agriculture saw the photographs that the researchers had collected, he "washed his hands of the whole affair" and the study was not published (1938, p. 51). The study Galpin refers to was apparently a study of New Madrid, Missouri, later mimeographed by Taylor as "Rich Man, Poor Man." There was, however, a way out of this difficulty. The location of rural sociologists in the Schools of Agriculture, which by this time were heavily reliant on statistical methods to assess the effectiveness of cropping methods, fertilizers, new strains, and so on, encouraged many rural sociologists of this generation to avoid the difficulties of reform politics through the pursuit of methodological rigor.

15. The first editor was a Chapin student, and the intellectual leadership of the separated field, which was statistical in its orientation, included other Chapin students. Thus rural sociology preserved and improved the statistical tradition during the interwar period. The separation of the field meant that it could not serve as a model, however, at least while alternative conceptions of sociology were heavily funded by foundations or attracted students.

16. The origins of the key participants are instructive. Paradoxically, although Chicago was a major beneficiary of the Rockefeller grants, the ideas that were carried by these grants, and especially the enormous SSRC grants, were

the ideas of Columbia quantitative social science of the prewar period. Among the sociologists in the SSRC, Giddings's students dominated: Ogburn, Chapin, and Gillin each served on the Counsel in the 1920s, as did Mayo-Smith's student Willcox, and Ogburn continued to serve until 1941. Rice was a staff member in the 1930s, and Chapin headed one of the Council's larger projects, *Social Science Abstracts*. Merriam himself was, of course, Columbia trained, and the SSRC was in part an extension of his personal network. Although the organization always had the support of Chicago, and although the organization expanded within its first years to include representatives of the American Statistical, Psychological, Anthropological, and Historical Associations, the Columbia stamp was always evident. The staff included ex-Columbia faculty, such as the historian Shotwell; its larger enterprises, such as the *Encyclopedia of the Social Sciences*, were controlled by old Columbians, such as E. R. A. Seligman; within the Council as representatives of societies or as council-selected at-large members, the Columbia sociologists routinely found their former teachers at Columbia, such as Wesley Claire Mitchell and E. C. Hayes; and the representation of the American Statistical Association, which was also dominated by Columbia sociology, often included Columbians, such as Ogburn and F. A. Ross, editor of the *Journal of the American Statistical Association* and for many years statistics instructor, with Chaddock, in the sociology department.

17. At a time when he was stung by a journalist's article in *Harper's* titled "The Great Fact-finding Farce," Ogburn insisted to Wesley Claire Mitchell that "we are not just finding facts. We are organizing them, drawing conclusions, and interpreting them in the scientific sense of the word" (quoted in Bannister, 1987, p. 184). These slogans were insufficient, and he found himself in disagreement, particularly with Merriam, over just what was and was not admissible under the heading of "science." This was doubtless part of the background to the essay "Limitations of Statistics," which he published in the *AJS* in the following year and which presents an extremely restricted conception of what can be "scientifically" known in social science.

18. In 1929, a subcommittee of the Committee on Social and Economic Research in Agriculture was established, producing recommendations for the requirement of two or three semester courses in mathematics as a prerequisite for statistics. Moreover, it recommended additional calculus requirements for students in economic theory in anticipation of a future in which social scientists would need greater mathematical skill (Sibley, 1974, pp. 21-22). In 1928 another committee, on the measurement of attitudes and public opinion, was established.

19. Lynd was not alone in entering sociology through the side door. Robert MacIver was another person with no "professional" background in sociology, entering the New York scene from a teaching position in Toronto as an evaluator of a Rockefeller-supported project in the reduction of intergroup tensions and staying on as a Barnard professor. MacIver chose Lynd for the position at Columbia rather than any product or member of a ranked sociology department. MacIver later recalled that at the time he was given control over the department, sociology was still viewed as something of a midwestern aberration (RMI)—a crippling perception in a city that held itself to be a model of enlightenment and advanced thinking. What both groups wanted was someone

less troublesome ("rambunctious" was MacIver's term) than Giddings, a critic of large corporations and a self-defined defender of the middleclass.

Harvard in the 1930s and 1940s presents a similar picture. "Sociology" as defined by the American Sociological Society did not exist, and when the department was established in the 1930s, it had as "members" such nonsociologists as the Pareto follower Henderson. Henderson was ultimately followed by Parsons and Homans, who were also nonsociologists by training. Neither had, as Lynd had had, any public reputation whatever at the time they became Harvard "sociologists." Sorokin and Zimmerman were both from a ranked department, Minnesota, but they were relatively powerless in the ducal Harvard system.

20. Newell Sims, author of one of the three prewar "community studies" dissertations under Giddings, later dismissed Clark Wissler's "specious claim" about the originality of the book's application of the anthropological method to an American community (quoted in Nelson, 1969, p. 213), maintaining that he and Williams had used similar "methods." What is revealing is that Lynd could so easily ignore these earlier efforts, primarily because the audiences with which he dealt in New York were sufficiently different and far removed from the audience of disciplinary sociology that claims about originality could be made without fear of contradiction. The same pattern, as we will see, holds in sociological theory.

21. An interesting organizational account of the process of transformation of the reform impulse in social work is Frank Weed's "Bureaucratization as Reform" (1979). A more personal account, which tells something of the relations of sociologists to the process, is E. T. Devine's *When Social Work Was Young* (1939).

22. The APSA had similar conflicts, with some of the same consequences, but the differences are striking. The journal of the APSA was run throughout this period and into the 1950s by a "managing editor," each of whom served for a very long period of time. P. A. Ogg served in this capacity for almost a quarter century, though not without criticism, especially in the 1930s at the same time that the *AJS* came under attack. In both cases, one underlying reason for the criticisms must have been the relatively new phenomenon of rejection. When his editorial work came under attack in the early 1940s, Ogg defended his rejection of half the submissions by remarking on the number of manuscripts being submitted by younger and less experienced scholars and observing that specialty journals were drawing away some of the better manuscripts (Somit and Tanenhaus, 1982, p. 97).

23. The SRA has been misdescribed as a Chicago-dominated organization. It would be more accurate, but still quite insufficient, to say that it was the old FHG Club writ large. Giddings's students and the students of his students, such as Chapin's student George Lundberg, dominated the organization numerically and had the greatest stake in its continuation before World War II. But they successfully gained the participation of such major figures in the Chicago empirical tradition as Burgess and attempted to co-opt a few others, such as Sorokin and later Parsons. The aim of the organization was to promote the "scientific" approach to sociology, and, in the early years, the group met in a special session to discuss, in a freer and more open fashion than the formal

sessions of the ASS, important topics relating to research methods. The timing of the organization of this group is significant: it took up where the SSRC attempts at reaching unanimity through conference discussions left off. It was primarily an attempt to mark the boundaries of a new disciplinary elite, however, and it continued to perform this function in the period after World War II.

24. This statement, in response to Chapin's criticism of Columbia and Chicago for overproducing Ph.D.'s was utopian: no significant demand existed at the time in the kinds of municipal agencies Faris believed should employ sociologists. Faris was not the last leader of a large Ph.D. program to refuse to reduce Ph.D. production in the face of an adverse employment picture. Indeed, the structure of the University of Chicago made the department totally dependent on graduate enrollments and grants, so that Faris had little choice. The graduates themselves sometimes did take positions in the federal government as statisticians or demographers, but most of the excess was absorbed into the unexpected expansion of demand for Ph.D. holders in the colleges and the continued expansion of undergraduate teaching.

25. Odum's *American Sociology* (1951) has a series of lists of texts in each of these areas. His own textbook contributions to the social problems literature included his *Man's Quest for Social Guidance* (1927) and *American Social Problems* (1939). The sociologists of the generation trained before the 1920s were devoted to the genre: virtually all of Giddings's students, for example, wrote textbooks, and sometimes they wrote several.

26. The discipline that made the greatest effort at producing a methodological consensus had the greatest failure. Merriam organized three National Conferences on the Science of Politics from 1923 to 1925; the movement then built to the end of the decade, but "receded almost overnight" and by the early 1930s was not a factor (Somit and Tanenhaus, 1982, p. 87). The situation of the field was, however, different in crucial respects: the traditional tasks of critical analysis of legislation and the history of legislation, the history of political philosophy, and other such activities could neither be readily subsumed into some sort of statistical "science" of politics, nor could they be readily delegitimated as activities. So there was no prospect for the discipline drawing its boundaries in a way that excluded these activities. Merriam himself, speaking of the historical-comparative and legalistic approaches to politics, said that "I am not suggesting that we ask our older friends to go" (quoted in Somit and Tanenhaus, 1982, pp. 110-111).

In sociology, however, the aim was precisely to exclude "philosophy" in favor of "science." But the sociologists had as much trouble as the political scientists in coming to terms on a coherent conception of "science." The SSRC sponsored one major attempt to construct a consensual methodological position for the social sciences, a volume edited by Stuart Rice (1931) containing critical studies of exemplary pieces of social research from all the discipline and problem areas of the empirical social sciences. There was no heavy-handed attempt to integrate the results; it had become apparent from the first that there was so much diversity that even such tasks as the selection of lists of important recent works caused serious disagreement. The member associations of the SSRC were polled to ask them to provide lists for their discipline of "ten outstanding contributions." Only the ASS complied before the plans were changed, and the list was so heterogeneous (ranging from *The Protestant Ethic* to statistician and economist Mordecai Ezekiel's dissertation work on curvilinear multiple correlation methods) that no strongly coherent message was transmitted by the selection, and certainly not the message that the SSRC wished to transmit. As Rice ruefully remarks in the appendix in which this list appears, "it gives evidence of the difficulty of making a selection of 'outstanding contributions' unless criteria of 'significance' or 'importance' are themselves agreed upon in advance." And, he went on, "These criteria will depend on a point of view, and will be arbitrary" (1931, p. 749).

27. Floyd House (1936) contrasted two kinds of responses to the discussion of fundamental issues in the logic of sociology, the history of sociology, and sociological theory. At the extreme was an "American sociologist of considerable prestige and influence [who] makes no secret of his opinion that questions of sociological theory and logic, and the history of the subject, are of so little importance, in comparison with specific research problems, that no time should be allotted to these topics in a sound program of studies for candidates for higher degrees in sociology" (p. 301). The streak of anti-intellectualism behind these attitudes was very visible. Ellwood quotes the slogan "don't think, observe!" (1933, p. 26). A more moderate form of this opinion, stated by Malcolm Willey in a session on teaching sociology at the ASS meetings, was that "students who expect to become professional sociologists should be directed to begin their graduate studies with concrete research and should acquire their grasp of sociological theory by a spontaneous exploration of the literature that they find necessary to illuminate the research problems with which they are concerned" (characterized in House, 1936, p. 301). The term *concrete research* was a code word associated with the SSRC. Ellwood quotes a commonplace of the day to the effect that the motto of the SSRC was "Millions for concrete research, but not one cent for philosophy" (1933, p. 26).

28. The issues were thoroughly entangled. Ellwood's own position was part of a constellation of ideas about the relation of sociology to values and public purposes that owed a great deal to his teachers, Dewey and Mead, and to Ward's idea of an edifying sociology. Ellwood argued that not only are sociologists citizens, with the duties of citizens, but that "While the scholar must preserve the detached and impersonal view in the study of human affairs . . . he should never lose touch with the actual, concrete human world," and it is perhaps best if this is done "through actual participation" (1933, pp. 9-10). He extended this to the writings of sociology itself by arguing that one objection to behaviorism was that "it states its results in language unintelligible except to the initiated," a criticism made relevant by Ellwood's view that "the social sciences can never be of much utility until their conclusions are understood, accepted, and acted upon by the mass of common men" (p. 53). This was not a crank perception of the purposes of the field. One finds Percy Bridgman assuming the same conception of sociology as an edifying discipline in his debate with Samuel Stouffer in 1950 (SAS) but he comes to the opposite conclusion: man is insufficiently rational to be helped by sociology; in a sense, this was Ellwood's own later conclusion when he decided that Christianity would have to provide for the needs of the world for moral and intellectual guidance.

29. The strategy Eubank employs is to build up a synthetic framework of concepts beginning with the act, and building, through the role of group life in the satisfaction of desires, toward the role of group life in (1) shaping volition, (2) controlling actions, and (3) "providing the culture in which his life is set and by which it is conditioned" (1932, p. 389).

30. If one compares the topical range of early Parsonian sociology to the range of topics taken up in a typical introductory text of the 1930s—say, the collaborative work by Jerome Davis and Harry Elmer Barnes (1931)—it is evident that Parsons's main weapon in bringing order to the problems of sociology was to exclude most of the traditional topics. In this text the topics included climate, public health, heredity and race, geographical influences, prehistorical human development, social psychology, leadership and propaganda, culture patterns, the social heritage, culture areas, social organization, the community and the state, the capitalist order, poverty, crime, the home, leisure, and so forth.

31. His student A. A. Tenney recalled this in a memorial essay published in 1931 (Odum, 1951, p. 93).

32. Lynd, writing in the late 1930s of the students in graduate programs in sociology, observed

> that graduate departments of history, like similar departments of sociology, and for the same reason, draw an unduly large number of students of undefined or miscellaneous interests. One does not require a defined interest in a problem singled out and seen in relation to other problems in order to "go in for" history or sociology. These fields are so broad that they seem especially inviting for the student who goes in, wanders around, and hopes in some mysterious way to "find himself"—and in the course of this to find a career. In this respect history and sociology are not simply unfortunate victims of circumstance. It is the amorphous character of both disciplines that attracts to them the amorphous student. ([1939] 1967, p. 174)

THREE

The New Optimism: American Sociology After World War II

The postwar situation was greatly influenced by the peculiar academic demography of the period and an equally peculiar excess of demand for certain kinds of research product. In terms of demography, the 15 years from the beginnings of the Depression to the end of the war effectively cut off the process of reproduction. Jobs were scarce; some of the best and brightest products of departments like Chicago—Abe Jaffe for example—took government rather than academic positions. Yet the exceptions are interesting: Samuel Stouffer, David Riesman, Arnold Rose, William Sewell, Paul Lazarsfeld, Talcott Parsons, Herbert Blumer, and Robert Merton all became active "sociologists" during this period. By the end of the war, they found themselves in a discipline with its earlier generation of "leaders" at or near retirement age. Giddings had been more prolific as a teacher of Ph.D.'s in the decade before World War I, when he was in his late 40s and early 50s. His students—Stuart Chapin, William F. Ogburn, John Gillin, Frank Hamilton Hankins, and Howard Odum—had built their careers in a period when the rise of Ph.D.'s had ceased and the academic job market was collapsing. In the 1930s, many faculty members were forced to take salary cuts, and few positions were available. Between 1930 and 1945,

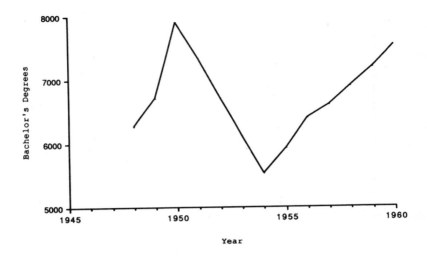

Figure 3.1. Sociology Bachelor's Degrees 1948 to 1960

membership in the ASS fell almost by half. When the postwar G.I. Bill changed these trends dramatically, these leaders were either professors emeriti or near retirement.

Thus, as sociology enrollments expanded (see Figure 3.1, 3.2, and 3.3), a new demographic resource was available, but the capacity to respond to the opportunity was diminished. As a result, some unusual patterns of recruitment to sociology could be observed. This recruitment was to have a significant effect on sociology because the postwar era marked the beginning of the rapid growth of sociology, as evidenced by student enrollments, membership in ASS (see Figure 3.4), and access to new sources of research funds.

When universities like Columbia and Harvard sought to expand their offerings in the 1940s and to replace lost, dead, or retired faculty, they did so by reaching beyond the established disciplinary hierarchy in sociology. At Columbia, for example, Chaddock's position was divided between Robert Merton, whose full professorship at 32 was sponsored by Robert MacIver,

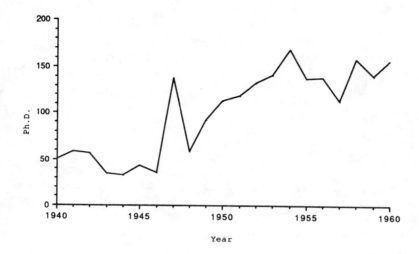

Figure 3.2. Sociology Ph.D.'s 1940 to 1960

and Paul Lazarsfeld (the latter being in no sense a sociologist at this time and who was personally sponsored by Robert Lynd, an individual separated from the intellectual traditions of sociology). Merton's Harvard background made him an outsider, especially judged by the standards of the discipline that had been created by Giddings's students, to which MacIver[1] was fundamentally hostile, or by Chicago norms. At Harvard, the situation was made unusual by the role of Henderson, a biologist and follower of Vilfredo Pareto, who had great influence as a campus "broker." Henderson had an appointment in sociology, and he saw to it that George Homans, a member of the Boston social elite, was named to a position in sociology. Homans had never been exposed to the existent sociological tradition, save for his relationship with Henderson's "Pareto Circle" and his participation in the Western Electric studies. Talcott Parsons, who had become a member of the sociology department in 1931 and was still an assistant professor at the start of the war, capitalized on local Harvard circumstances and Sorokin's poor reputation with the

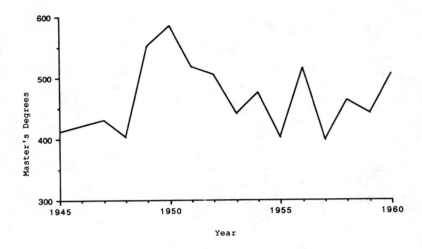

Figure 3.3. Sociology Master's Degrees 1948 to 1960

Harvard aristocracy to create a new department, Social Relations. Even at Chicago, the department had difficulty reproducing itself. Leo Goodman was brought into the department as a statistician with the hope that he would learn sociology on the job; David Riesman, whose *The Lonely Crowd* (1950) made him famous, was recruited to the undergraduate College and was involved in the Community and Family Studies Center and in the community study in Kansas City, which was perhaps the largest of its type in the postwar era. Among the Europeans who secured academic positions were Hans Gerth and Alfred Schutz.

One issue raised by these recruitments into the best universities is the apparent fragility of the theoretical and methodological traditions of sociology. How could it happen, one might ask, that 50 years after the first degrees in sociology were granted; amateurs could rise to central positions in sociology? The question is more complex than it at first appears, and can be answered only by taking yet other issues into account. The fact that most of the major departments of sociology were in the Midwest or the South

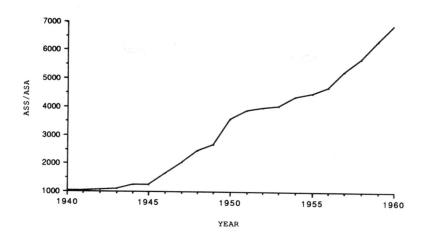

Figure 3.4. ASS/ASA Membership 1940 to 1960

was one central reason. During the interwar years, and to a lesser extent afterwards, the faculties of Ivy League universities were virtually impermeable to midwesterners, westerners, and southerners who had not at least passed through "socially appropriate" academic institutions. The snobbism of these institutions took a particular form: foreigners and even Jews, whose entry into many of these universities was still regulated by an informal quota system, were less threatening to the status-anxious leaders of these universities than the graduates of the state universities[2] and, as a consequence, they fared better than the indigenous faculty of other regions.

In terms of research, a postwar expansion of funding created a lag between the supply of sociologists and the demand for researchers in large team operations. Virtually all of the figures who rose from the margins to the center of sociology in this period did so on the basis of significant funded research. The character of the funding atmosphere is thus an essential part of the story of the change. The effects of the unusual demand situation were striking and, in several respects, destructive to the academic traditions that had been established, particularly to the remnants of the reform mentality that still dominated sociology in the 1930s.

FOUNDATIONS AND THE NEW ACADEMIC HIERARCHY

The relations of foundations to the sociological profession touring the immediate postwar period were radically unlike the ones that had existed in the early 1930s. Quite apart from the situation of sociology itself, these new relations had significant effects on the rankings of universities in the American academic hierarchy. Both processes of change had prewar roots, and the changes cannot be precisely dated. Columbia and Harvard were major beneficiaries of new funding by foundations during the postwar period. Harvard changed from being a college of the national political elite and Boston gentry to an ambitious university, competing for the best graduate students in academic disciplines.

The transformation of the Ivy League is a complex story that is not complete even today. Suffice it to say that the whole model of graduate school dominance established at Johns Hopkins, Columbia, and Chicago by the late 19th century had only slowly been adopted by the Ivy League schools, which considered undergraduate training to be their primary mission. Moreover, they often paid very poorly on the assumption that a professor was already well-to-do, or, if he was not, should be able to translate the prestige of his appointment into a match with a suitably rich and acceptable bride. Harvard in the 1920s and 1930s was still in part governed by social as much as academic standards: publication was not essential to respectability, and indeed the primary vehicle of scholarly publication in sociology during the interwar years, textbooks, was considered *infra dignitatum*. The roots of the changes that transformed Harvard were deep and date at least from the presidency of Charles Eliot at the turn of the century. Foundations were essential to the change and financed parts of it. Even by the 1920s, the university had demonstrated a great affinity for foundations, which were often run from New York club circles in which Harvard's friends and graduates were well represented. From the mid-1930s on, Harvard's transformation, heavily funded by a Rockefeller grant on "industrial hazards," began to affect sociology at Harvard, and ultimately the rankings and relations of sociology departments nationally (Buxton and Turner, 1990).

In the state universities, there was greater continuity. Two of the top five sociology departments in the mid-1930s were in state universities of the Midwest, the universities of Wisconsin and Minnesota. Minnesota, dominated by Giddings's students, produced what was to be the leadership of rural sociology, a sub-discipline relatively unaffected by the cutbacks of the Depression. Among Chapin's students were T. Lynn Smith, Charles Lively, and B. O. Williams, who were ultimately to head departments at such universities as Louisiana State, Florida, Ohio State, Missouri, and the huge department at Georgia, and to hire like-minded statistical sociologists. But the changes of the postwar era reduced these departments, several of which were among the largest in the country, to regionally important or second or third-tier doctoral programs. In the postwar era, these departments expanded and absorbed many of the new Ph.D.'s, but in relative terms, with respect to prestige, they declined.

Rural sociology, funded differently and organized into units with a different relationship to the university as a whole, separated itself from the rest of sociology, especially after the founding of the journal *Rural Sociology* in 1936. The sources of support for rural research in the 1930s did not expand as quickly as other sources for nonrural departments and operated in terms of patronage vehicles that were now becoming outdated: small projects that did not require large staffs of specially trained research personnel. Moreover, the social research activities of the Department of Agriculture, always politically fragile, came under attack immediately after the war.[3]

The grant program, or more properly the research support, that existed under the agricultural research station system in the

1930s is a familiar model in world science. The stations were in effect "institutes" dedicated to broadly practical purposes with a great deal of autonomy in selecting research topics. There were limitations, notably those arising from the limited resources available and the service ethic that governed their allocation. There were also political limitations that arose from the cooperative character of the financing of these institutes, which were funded partly by the federal government, partly by states. Sociology had a secondary role in this kind of institute, and often sociologists felt that they had to prove their value by adhering very closely to the aims of the research stations and by respecting the political realities of their funding. These intangible limitations were sometimes very severe. In the natural sciences, this model of institute control was heavily criticized, especially during the period of negotiations over the form that postwar funding for science would take (one proposal had the government setting up science institutes, connected to state universities). The argument made by the scientists was that the "research proposal system," which had grown up in the practice of private foundations rather than government science, was better suited than giant state research institutes to the preservation of the investigators' creativity and intellectual freedom.

Of course relations with the foundations were themselves restrictive, but in different and less routinized ways. Where rural sociologists had to persuade a politically sensitive dean of a school of agriculture or an experiment station director on the merits of their research, the kind of grant that was crucial for the postwar era required sociologists to persuade a foundation officer or businessman to support research. This more difficult task was eased by various new circumstances, including the gradual working out of models of research that patrons and sociologists both found valuable. Over time, there evolved a community of like-minded foundation officers and sociologists.

The story of the emergence of foundations as a powerful force in academic social science is both complex and open to alternative interpretations. As we have seen, the early relations of the Rockefeller Foundation with the social sciences were intrusive and overbearing, especially for the social scientists who had to puzzle out just what was expected of them. The character of the relations changed as a result of the expanded role of such Rockefeller intermediaries as Beardsley Ruml, a social scientist *manqué* who was perhaps the first in a large class of foundation officers who served as advisors and employees of New York foundations. In time, especially after the death of the persons directly associated with the millionaire who had endowed the foundations, this kind of work became a career, with its own hierarchy, kinds of achievement, and imperatives of competition. A smaller foundation, like the Carnegie, would pride itself on the innovative character of the work it supported, and to do so it would need to employ persons capable of putting together projects and applicants who could carry out the projects. The kinds of broad and simple-minded goals of the 1920s did not suffice; now what made a foundation officer's reputation was his successes in organizing. What destroyed this reputation was financing a disaster or activities that exposed the foundation to public embarrassment and criticism. Organizations like the SSRC and the appearance of control by professionals served an important purpose in insulating the foundations from unwelcome regulation, criticism, or political scrutiny. Frederick Keppel, long-time head of the Carnegie Corporation, tellingly referred to them as "buffer states."

To succeed in the role of foundation officer required a good sense of what could be accomplished and who could accomplish it. In the case of social research, success required close personal relations with the "establishment" that had developed around the activities of the SSRC. Discretion, good judgment, and an appropriate range of personal contacts to get sound advice were the characteristics essential to the work of the good foundation officer. These same characteristics were also essential for administration and those universities that depended on philanthropy, such as Harvard and Columbia. As a result, there was often an exchange of personnel between universities and philanthropic organizations. Robert Lynd served in each kind of organization; Beardsley Ruml, the Rockefeller figure, became a dean at Chicago. In the 1940s these kinds of exchanges increased, especially

94 THE IMPOSSIBLE SCIENCE

between Harvard and the New York foundations. Certain sociologists, such as Samuel Stouffer—hard-drinking and candid to friends as well as foundation and SSRC leaders but distant to the discipline at large—became major "informants" for the philanthropic community. These "broker" roles were crucial to the emerging patronage system, and the competitive character of the foundation world of the 1940s changed the once leisurely pace of foundation activity. Moreover, the potential social science grantees had alternative funding sources that they could play off against one another—other foundations, government and business.

The decision to finance particular research projects in these agencies was highly personalistic: few systematic mechanisms, such as formal peer review of proposals, were employed by the agencies, and as a result, a strong personal bond often developed between a rising bureaucrat in the agencies and an academic or survey research institute research entrepreneur (Young, 1948, p. 330). This bond, in turn, allowed research ideas to develop and their financing to be approved with a minimum of bureaucratic difficulty and scrutiny from the profession of social researchers.

The concept of "project grants" itself was a product of the 1930s: the Rockefeller practice of the 1920s was to provide "block" or relatively unrestricted grants for capital improvements, particularly buildings, and for unspecified research to be distributed at the discretion of committees or institute officers within a university. In contrast, the use of project grants shifted power back into the hands of the foundations, but required larger staff operations and greater internal expertise for the foundations. The method was first used in the mid-1930s by Warren Weaver, director of the Rockefeller Foundation's grant program in experimental biology. Social science followed in the next decade (Geiger, 1986, p. 165). The idea for *An American Dilemma* (Myrdal, 1962) was partly a "project" grant, partly a "commission." It used academics, but was not based in a university. Gunnar Myrdal, the director of the study and the author of the report, was chosen by the Carnegie Corporation, and the Corporation provided much of the administrative support that a university would otherwise have provided.

There was a considerable degree of disagreement within the philanthropic community about the efficacy of the project system. It was recognized, especially after the experience of the late 1940s, that there were dangers in large amounts of money being granted on the say-so of a very small community of academics and officers. A 1949 report of the Ford Foundation, the largest new entrant into the foundation world, observed that

> the university professor who takes such a project to a foundation is caught in a web of continuous negotiations with foundation officers, with the university administration, and with his colleagues in the professional societies and research councils on whose advice the foundation officers rely. In short, he is enmeshed in a kind of academic politics, and spends a great deal of time campaigning for his next year's grants instead of teaching, studying, or carrying on research. (Ford Foundation, 1949, pp. 109-110)

The character of the scholarly life was thus dramatically changed: dependence on the approval of one's professional peers, which had to be affirmed explicitly and frequently, became the new condition of scholarly competition.

For a time, competition strengthened the hands of both the intermediaries, who now possessed valuable contacts, and researchers who could now find alternative sources of funding but who were quite willing to exchange their reviews of others' projects for favorable treatment on their own. A powerful network of friendships, based in large part on the exchange of information and judgments about individuals' capacities to carry out foundation aims, developed between members of the social science establishment, especially among those who summered in New Hampshire, and the officers of foundations.

In the postwar period, these connections were put to work in support of "basic" social science research, the prestige of which had increased during the war. The evolution from the hybrid models of research financing of the 1920s and 1930s was slow, and never quite complete, but the changes were nonetheless dramatic. The number of sponsors of research increased, and, as a result, the de facto monopoly exercised by the Rockefeller staff disappeared.[4] These conditions lasted only a short period—perhaps for five years after World War II. The community of foundation officers and relatively young, highly ambitious sociologists fresh from their wartime successes thrived during the period because of the shared sense of a great common task and because several foundations were willing to finance these visions. Power was distributed rather oddly during this era, however. Although the foundation officers were dependent on the personal advice of trusted social scientists, they were very powerful figures and could make very sharp personal judgments about grantees and the conditions under which grants would be given. In one notorious instance, foundation officers pronounced H. Stuart Hughes politically unacceptable for a position as administrator of the Russian Research Center at Harvard. Harvard's administrators complied, including Talcott Parsons who was on the board of the Center. In other cases, foundations were quietly consulted by the administrators of leading eastern universities about the acceptability of proposed administrative appointments. Yet the foundation leadership was not inclined to engage in what was characterized negatively as "retail philanthropy," so it was compelled to give large grants and rely on personal connections with leading sociologists and academic administrators to assess proposals for research projects.

This system at first benefited only the large private universities. Public universities generally could not commit resources and make decisions quickly enough to respond to the challenge, and only when the pattern of grant funding in the natural sciences was well established did they become able to do so. Chicago, Harvard, and Columbia became the universities most able to compete; other universities with similar advantages, such as Ivy League universities that were without sociology departments, or which had only modest departments, became important competitors to the older departments, or created institutes that performed social research. The emergence of a conventional research form by the middle of the 1950s dissipated these advantages and set the stage for the spectacular proliferation of empirical research of the 1960s. This research, however, was funded in a way that contrasted in several important respects to the *gemeinschaftliche* community of the foundations. Agencies of the federal government increasingly operated under systems of peer reviews, and this shifted control into the hands of academics. Moreover, the diversity of government funding sources permitted different academic factions within the discipline to find funding homes.

TRANSITIONAL ORGANIZATIONAL FORMS

A brief history of "patronage vehicles" in sociology is needed to understand the changes that took place. From the 1860s on, the idea of a commission to study a problem, make a diagnosis, and propose solutions had been the central patronage vehicle for research that involved sociologists. The standard form was this: a "problem," as identified in public discussion, would be assigned to some investigative authority or body, either public or private. The *American Dilemma* (Myrdal, 1962) study, performed during the war, was in a sense the last of this old type of project, and its history may be used to fix our bearings on the changed relations of social scientists to foundations. The project employed several sociologists, such as the young Arnold Rose, Edward Shils, and the ubiquitous Stouffer, among others, in a study that addressed a basic social problem. Notably, it was one of the problems that was taboo for rural sociologists. Indeed, it was a problem that scuttled U.S. Department of Agriculture social research and served as an obstacle to the inclusion of the social sciences under the National Science Foundation. The *American Dilemma* study was conceived not by academics but by foundation officers who sought academics to perform it. By this time, of course, a network of reputable advisors existed on which the foundation officers could draw. In this case they listened, but were very far from being bound by what they heard. The Carnegie Corporation was not as rich as the Rockefeller Foundation and was at a crucial stage of development. Some of the older employees could speak with authority about the donor's original intention, but this number was dwindling. As a consequence, internal conflicts over aims could only be resolved by greater initiative on the part of the newer officers, who began to establish a philanthropic agenda of their own, employ staff who fit the agenda, and create bonds of trust with academics who could be relied upon to give relatively disinterested advice on ideas for projects and on the merits of potential grantees.

The idea behind the study came from a trustee of the foundation, Newton Baker, a former mayor of Cleveland and secretary of war under Woodrow Wilson. The social connections here are illustrative. Frederick Keppel, who had been dean of Columbia College, the men's undergraduate school of Columbia University, and who had served as assistant to Baker as secretary of war, had been president of the Carnegie Corporation since 1923. Frederick Keppel, Jr., became an assistant to General Frederick Osborne during the Second World War, and then a Harvard Administrator. The Corporation had traditionally supported black colleges, but Keppel and Baker wished to do something more dramatic, and Baker's idea of a comprehensive study of the race question appealed to Keppel. They considered American scholars who might undertake the task and decided that "Americans, both black and white, had too many prejudices to write an objective and fresh study" (Southern, 1987, p. 4). They settled on Gunnar Myrdal, who was a scholar from a European country without imperialist interests and who had experience in the United States, having had a Rockefeller fellowship in 1929-1930. Myrdal was reluctant, but Beardsley Ruml, who had headed the program that had brought the Myrdals to the United States earlier, visited the Myrdals in Sweden and persuaded them to accept. The price Myrdal demanded was high, and the study itself was very lavishly financed.

There was some resentment among American scholars at Myrdal's selection, especially since Myrdal's views differed from the dominant traditions in the study of race relations, which stressed the relative immutability of fundamental attitudes and rejected the prosperity for "social engineering" in the face of these attitudes. Yet the new social psychology of Herbert Blumer, as well as of the attitude researchers of the day, now stressed the relative lack of influence of traditional values on action and suggested that the determinants of social behavior were the potentially manipulable features of the group environments in which the individuals found themselves. The belief in the malleability of attitudes was one justification of their study, and the survey research that was concerned with attitudes was premised on the idea of mutable attitudes to action. Thus, Myrdal's book had a potentially receptive audience, in spite of its apparent hostility to the race relations tradition. Moreover, Myrdal co-opted many of the younger figures in American sociology by employing them to write reports on specific topics. He dealt with elder sociologists with the same intent: reports were commissioned from dozens of social scientists, and the Carnegie Corporation paid well for them and for his American "research assistants."

The written form of the study was also transitional: a mixture of edification, which was the primary aim of the Carnegie Corporation sponsoring the study, and an analytic study that followed the theme of the "dilemma" between American public ideals of rationalistic egalitarianism and the realities of conduct involving blacks. The study included some history as well as economic, demographic, and institutional analyses of the situation of blacks in the South. The crux of the argument related to attitudes. Myrdal was aware of the quantitative literature on racial attitudes that had developed in the 1930s and did not deny the value of questionnaire data. However, the bulk of the book is an informal analysis of the ideational structure of southern racial ideology as it was realized in practice. In fact, Myrdal specifically avoided the use of the terms *attitudes* and *prejudice* in favor of the concept of discrimination, "the objective aspect of prejudice" (1962, p. 1141). The extent to which Myrdal felt free to innovate theoretically and employ diverse methods is equally evident in the contemporaneous study of anti-Semitism sponsored by the American Jewish Committee, published under the title *The Authoritarian Personality* (Adorno, Frenkel-Brunswik, Levinson, and Sanford, 1950).

Soft-methods studies of wide scope were supported by foundations for the next few years, though it should be stressed that these funds were in effect available only to scholars who met certain criteria: the projects generally took place at a university that was socially tied to the New York foundation community and were directed by a person who had earned a place on the foundation officers' list of talented individuals. David Riesman, a lawyer by training and a former law school professor, was one major beneficiary of this system. Riesman's *The Lonely Crowd* (1950) was another Carnegie project, with a similar mix of edifying aims and informal, impressionistic methods. But the community of foundation officers and leading social scientists was clearly divided on the merits of these works, and it was evident that many of the sociologists and "behavioral scientists" who had been supported by, or involved with, the SSRC were actively hostile to this kind of work.

Foundation-supported research was often not research of the type done by Myrdal and Riesman, and as the 1950s progressed, this kind of project diminished in importance compared to survey research and quantitatively oriented social-psychological research, much of which was highly routinized. The "survey" became a new type of patronage vehicle, which was able to serve a variety of purposes and patrons. The classical survey research projects were those conducted by Lazarsfeld at the Bureau of Applied Social Research (BASR), but the structure of patronage for his projects was exceptional. Lazarsfeld was a mathematician by training, who had performed a number of survey research studies of a psychological type in Austria before coming to the United States as a Rockefeller fellow—a program that launched the American academic careers of a number of European emigrés in the 1930s. When he decided to stay in the United States, he continued to perform market research, which was developing rapidly as a nonacademic and primarily psychological form of inquiry during the 1920s. When a large grant was given to Princeton University in 1935 to study radio listening patterns, Lazarsfeld was engaged as the director of the project.

Lazarsfeld created the BASR to carry out those survey projects for which he could find funding. He first constructed an affiliation with the University of Newark, an institution with an ambitious president. In 1941, he moved the bureau to Columbia and negotiated a new arrangement. The arrangement was novel, and Lazarsfeld regarded the organizational aspects of the Bureau, which were copied elsewhere, to be one of his great achievements. The projects themselves were rather distinctive, especially during the prime of the Bureau in the 1940s and 1950s. The paradigmatic kind of project was a survey with a highly practical purpose tailored to the specific concerns of some business, which was funded at a sufficiently high level to enable Lazarsfeld to add material and talented helpers so as to conduct an academic research project at the same time. This was in some sense a novel approach. Works like those of the Institute for Social and Religious Research (ISRR) were designed to be simultaneously academic or sociological and to serve the practical aims of patrons. Lazarsfeld separated the two: for the patron he produced a report, while for the academic audience he produced books, typically coauthored by several participants who were employees of the Bureau (e.g., Lazarsfeld, Berelson, and Gaudet). Moreover, his students produced dissertations analyzing the data under his tutelage.

This strategy was possible only under some highly specific historical conditions that soon vanished. The funds necessary to support writing an academic book depended on the ability of Lazarsfeld to sell sponsors on what were, in effect, grossly overpriced survey projects. Once the survey research business itself advanced to the point that nonacademic competitors could undercut the prices Lazarsfeld had to charge, this kind of project was no longer marketable. Moreover, while it was in its prime, funding depended on Lazarsfeld's ability to make contacts and sell ideas, and on his proximity to corporate sources of funding. His long relationship with Frank Stanton of CBS and his close ties to the research side of the advertising business were also crucial to his success.[5] Lazarsfeld's practice was to give luncheon talks to corporate leaders, an activity for which there are endless opportunities. When one of the members of the audience remarked to him on some similar issue that had arisen in his own company, Lazarsfeld would arrange to have lunch with him and try to persuade him to fund a research project to study it.

The strategy was highly successful, though scarcely duplicatable. Lazarsfeld combined a set of personal talents—research, invention of ideas, organization, and salesmanship—that could not all be learned (Sills, 1987; Barton, 1982).[6] In any case, although other sociologists had opportunities to perform corporate work, few were situated close to the centers of corporate power. So the BASR system in this form could not flourish, at least on exactly the same terms. It was reproduced, for example, in California under Charles Glock, himself a former BASR director. But Glock's unit and the survey research units that many states established in the 1950s and 1960s were supported largely by federal grants, not by commercial work. Eventually Lazarsfeld himself decided that the commercial work was too much trouble, and he too switched to federal grants almost exclusively. By the end of the 1950s all of these units, as well as individual sociologists in academic sociology departments, were competing for sources from the same broad range of federal agencies.

Two other major survey research organizations were established in this period, both with wartime origins. The war had seen the rise of three government survey units concerned with morale, with each having a slightly different methodological style and seeing itself as competitive with respect to methods. One was the Research Branch of the Division of Morale of the U.S. Army, under Samuel Stouffer's direction and the supervision of a New York foundation insider, Frederick Osborne; another was the Surveys Division of the Office of War Information (the propaganda arm of the government), directed by the pollster Elmo Wilson; and the third was the Program Surveys of the U.S. Department of Agriculture, directed by Rensis Likert, a psychologist and later a leading organizational thinker (Converse, 1987, p. 163). Morale was understood to be a fundamental national issue. The First World War had left a deep sense of cynicism about the merit of joining in European wars, and President Roosevelt, along with the Eurocentric elite which shared his desire to involve the United States, was anxious to secure and assess the level of public support for entry into the war. This led to a sharp generational division. Anti-imperialism was one of the most deeply rooted political traditions in American sociology, and many members of the older generation of sociologists and social scientists were opposed to American entry and fearful of the garrison state that they believed would inevitably follow an expanded world role for the United States. Charles Ellwood was a bitter draft opponent, and George Lundberg, Harry Elmer Barnes, and Charles Beard were vocal critics both of the interventionist mood and of the interventionist world role of the United States after the war. W. F. Ogburn (Bannister, in press), Ellsworth Faris, and doubtless many others whose attitudes had been shaped by the experience of World War I and its aftermath were quietly sympathetic to these views.

The new establishment in sociology did not share them at all. Stouffer's military role is famous, and Talcott Parsons had been an early member of the group of Harvard faculty that had begun to study the international situation and consider the implications of an expanded American role and intervention in the war in Europe, and to serve as "expert" intellectual contributors to it (Buxton and Turner, 1990). Parsons, like the survey researchers, sought to attach his work to the problem of morale (Converse, 1987, p. 160; Buxton, 1985). In the last years of the war, a new problem was subject to survey analysis: the effect of bombing on enemy morale.[7] Each of these projects created significant personal networks that were important to the participants for many years afterwards. These networks centered on the overlapping areas of the social psychological, the demographic, and the statistical, and to some extent "culture and personality."

The private survey organizations that the wartime surveyors established included the Institute for Social Research (ISR) at the University of Michigan under Likert. The National Opinion Research Center (NORC), then located in Denver, had done survey work under contract for Wilson's Office of War Information unit during the war and, in 1948, expanded operations and moved to Chicago to form a formal relationship with the University of Chicago (Converse, 1987, pp. 173-174). Stouffer established a small Laboratory of Social Relations at Harvard, but used other organizations, such as the NORC, for large-scale data collection. Other veterans of the wartime effort returned to academic departments and followed up on the interdisciplinary ideas in their own departmental settings and, in one important case, in the agricultural research station system. These departmental beginnings were small, since departments were not equipped to perform large-scale surveys. But for reasons that will become evident, these were the beginnings of the research mode that was to become dominant in the 1960s and typify current empirical sociology in the United States.

At the time William Sewell began projects at the University of Wisconsin there were few university funds for social research, and it was only as a consequence of years of internal political effort within the university that social science research came to be treated as a legitimate beneficiary of the funding available within the university for research—which, at Wisconsin, was a relatively large pool. Federal funds were at first almost nonexistent; the survey operations of the government were shut down, largely as a result of congressional criticism of political polling work during the bitter election of 1944 (Converse, 1987, pp. 207-211).[8] But from the late 1940s on, survey work, and social science research generally, established itself in other federal research agencies, especially the National Institutes of Health and the National Institute of Mental Health. Social science was excluded from the National Science Foundation (NSF), but eventually won acceptance there as well.

The survey researchers, whose careers had been propelled by the huge infusion of war money, were the advocates of a particular strategy for sociology as a discipline. They became its most powerful expositors, formulating their vision in a series of programmatic texts that embodied three basic elements: the advocacy of particular immediate foci for the task of turning sociology into a science, the promotion of disciplinary reforms, and the delineation of new cognitive aims for the discipline. The primary focus of attention of these programmatic texts was not on the distant theoretical aims of the field, but on the practical conditions for achieving the proximate goals of the researchers and on a program for the improvement of methods, particularly measurement techniques. On this there was a great deal of consensus, whereas on the subject of the theoretical goals of the discipline there was very little agreement. The methodological program and the institutional reformation of the discipline were inseparable in the minds, as well as in the writings, of these strategists. Each involved a complex transformation.

THE STRATEGIC CENTRALITY OF MEASUREMENT

Much of the excitement of participants in social research in this era reflected their sense that the wartime effort had made a radical break with the past. In particular, Lazarsfeld promoted this idea and, in an important sense, he was correct: the kind of research performed by Lazarsfeld in the 1940s was not traditional "sociology," but rather a kind of individualistic analysis relying for the most part on "folk psychology" for its theory, statistical methods borrowed from applied psychology rather than the correlation and regression techniques favored by the Ogburn generation, and survey or questionnaire methods borrowed from polling and market research. If one wished to characterize this work in academic terms, it would be appropriately called sociologically (or demographically) informed applied psychology; the "sociological" element was the use of standard demographic information and surrogate measures for class in questionnaires. It was concerned with the analysis of ideas and their attitudes or utterances, something that Ogburn and his peers had generally resisted in favor of behavioral indices. In Lazarsfeld's own case, he had started with a kind of market research—termed "reasons analysis"—that he had developed in Vienna for the questionnaires were essentially attempts to ask why someone did something. Lazarsfeld's early studies in the United States were also of this type, but by the 1940s the emphasis had changed to attitude measurement and what he retrospectively saw as an overemphasis on "sampling, attitude measurement, and so on" (PFLW, p. 71).

This overemphasis had a prehistory in sociology, of course, in the efforts of Stouffer to apply Thorndike's methods and in the struggles of Chapin to adapt Allport's ideas. By the 1940s an intense competitive dynamic within a group consisting of Chapin's student Louis Guttman, Stouffer, and Likert had developed. New ideas were immediately put into practice by the well-financed, large-scale wartime survey research units that employed these researchers, and practice changed rapidly. It was natural to conclude that these changes signaled a coming breakthrough, and that the path to making sociology into a science was to be through the improvement of measurement.

The concentration on measurement, which was the source of major postwar grants from the RAND Corporation to Stouffer,[9] was central to his public programmatic statements and his applications and reports to the grantors. The basic thesis of these various statements is contained in a favorite analogy to the development of medicine:

> Just as research in the history of medicine has depended on the invention of instruments like the thermometer and the microscope, so the new social research depends and will increasingly depend on what some people deprecatingly call gadgets. A questionnaire, or an attitude test is a gadget. (Stouffer, Reply to Bridgman, 1948, SAS, p. 6)

Stouffer was quite willing to accept that the origins of these gadgets were in market research rather than sociology, but he believed that the use and improvement of these gadgets for the specific purposes of sociology was the best present strategy for the discipline.

This "emphasis," which Lazarsfeld later insisted (PFLW) was not driven by the demands of clients but by the internal demands of developing technique, had a number of consequences. The infusion of social psychological thinking, which was based on an atheoretical and experimentalist tradition, served to undermine the coherence of "sociological problems." In addition, the needs of clients dictated the direction of much research.[10] The elaboration of the methods themselves required and encouraged their users to employ ad hoc hypotheses that had no roots in the sociological tradition and certainly not in theory.

Stouffer's work reflected this change, in spite of the fact that he continued to think of the delinquency work done by Clifford Shaw and Henry McKay under the influence of Robert Park's idea of social areas as a kind of paradigm of good sociology (Stouffer, 1950, p. 359; see also Letter to Conant, 1947, SAS). Lazarsfeld neither shared this tacit sense of "what a sociological problem is" nor did his allegiances to the goal of making sociology rigorous bind him to the tradition. Indeed, for Lazarsfeld, and ultimately for many of the social researchers that he trained, the domain of empirical work was a separate domain, with its own rules and strategies that were not dependent on any particular vision of sociology as a theoretical discipline. Lazarsfeld himself did not believe that a theoretical sociology was a reasonable goal, because of the extreme complexity of the subject matter. At best, he thought a kind of psychology might be constructed on the basis of the survey analyses that he performed. Critics like Herbert Blumer, who took him to task for the nonsociological character of his work, were incomprehensible to him, for he saw questionnaire studies of individuals as the only kind of social research that could serve as a starting place for empirical inquiry.

THE NECESSITY OF DISCIPLINARY REFORM

Techniques of the kind developed in connection with the large surveys required, first and foremost, technicians. And thus the training of technically competent sociologists became the strategic focus of this community in its efforts to reform sociology. The Social Science Research Council (SSRC) commissioned a report on the education and recruitment of social scientists in response to the perception that the students attracted to the social sciences were less talented than those in the sciences and engineering. The report, by SSRC official Elbridge Sibley, suggested, reassuringly, that a reasonable proportion of the best students were drawn to the social sciences, but the large number of students in the social sciences created an unfavorable ratio of faculty to students, especially as compared to the sciences. Moreover, the bulk of the students in the social sciences were oriented toward careers as practitioners rather than researchers, even at the graduate level (Young, 1948, p. 326). It was recognized that these students could not be simply turned away, but they could be segregated from the genuine research students, who could then be given appropriate training. Unfortunately, the report said, even at the best universities, inadequate provision was made for research training. The SSRC attempted throughout the 1950s to remedy these perceived deficiencies by creating committees to prepare training material in methodology, to promote increased mathematics training for social science undergraduates, and to provide opportunities for advanced training in quantitative methods. In addition, there was a strenuous insistence on the upgrading of standards of research, which took the familiar form of arguing that the bulk of the membership in the professional associations of social science consisted of persons who were unqualified for research. And this fed the fear that the "over-expanded market for research knowledge of social behavior, if unchecked, must inevitably shake confidence in the value of the scientific approach to problems of social relations" (Young, 1948, p. 325).

The problem of unqualified researchers was the result of the evolution of methods. In the days of the social survey movement, the requisite technical skills were minimal; many prospective "sociologists" learned on the job and made substantial contributions. As Lazarsfeld and Stouffer emphasized endlessly, what was now needed were specialists with technical training. As a result, the construction of the required course sequences, especially in statistics, became more common, though even at the end of the 1950s many well-regarded departments had only minimal statistics requirements.

These lists of complaints were extended in various directions. The new-style sociologists often found, as the quantifiers at the ISRR had to learn earlier, that the public did not understand or particularly respect their achievements. The usual solution was to call for popularizers who could serve the social sciences as they had successfully served the natural sciences. Popularization was understood to be inappropriate for an ordinary researcher, for unless researchers have some special gift for popularization, it would be better "if they confine themselves to their proper tasks and write their esoteric research reports for each other" (Young, 1948, pp. 333-334). The idea of social engineering, which still remained as a central usage in the vocabulary of sociologists when they attempted to explain the promise of social research to outsiders and skeptics, became increasingly troublesome, as the training of practitioners in such areas as city planning expanded and as the necessity for socializing students into the new model of technical research made itself felt. Finally, of course, there was the ever present problem of patrons' or clients' expectations. Although the postwar era saw a remarkable expansion of funding for basic research, especially in methodology, most of the funds for the large survey research organizations were tied to client needs that could not easily be reconciled with the disciplinary aims of sociology.

PROGRAMMATIC MODELS OF THE COGNITIVE AIMS OF SOCIAL SCIENCE

The 1940s and early 1950s were periods of relative tolerance with respect to fundamental methodological issues. The compromise between the Chicago "case study" practitioners and the Columbia quantifiers that led to the Sociological Research Association (SRA) held until the purging of the soft methods people in the Chicago department in the mid-1950s, after the death of Louis Wirth. One consequence of the formal basis for the compromise, the agreement that sociology was a "natural science," was that the issues were not stated in "philosophical" terms. The "soft" researchers, such as Riesman, simply viewed the conflict in terms of style and personalities, rather than as fundamental issues over the character of sociology, a topic which for him, as a person not formally trained in the field, had little salience. Both the Chicago school and the followers of Lazarsfeld and Merton adhered to a tabooing of methodological polemics. By the same token, as we have seen, there was a conscious refusal on the part of Stouffer and others to engage publicly in the kinds of methodological polemics that George Lundberg and Charles Ellwood had formulated in the 1930s. This suppression of methodological dispute became a convention among the well connected and increasingly became institutionalized as a disciplinary value, especially within the elite departments. Virtually no examples of methodological or philosophical polemics may be found coming from these departments after MacIver's *Social Causation* (1942). The writings of the marginalized Sorokin (1937) are the exception that proves the rule. What replaced this kind of writing, during the postwar period, was a different kind of text, the programmatic theoretical statement.

Parsons's formulation of these issues dating from the late 1940s, is especially striking, if only because of its startling aggressiveness:

> Social science is a going concern; the problem is not one of creating it, but rather of using and developing it. Those who still argue whether the scientific study of social life is possible are far behind the times. It is here, and that fact ends the argument. (1986, p. 107)

Donald Young, writing as head of the Russell Sage Foundation, made the same point: from the social scientists' point of view this is a dead issue (1948, p. 334). These were nevertheless merely tactical assertions. In fact, the legitimacy of the social sciences' claims to the status of science was constantly under attack or subject to a corroding skepticism. The hearings and programmatic pronouncements by natural scientists that led up to the creation of the NSF showed unequivocally that many natural scientists simply rejected the scientific pretensions of the social sciences and refused to be associated with them.

Even Stouffer, who was unwilling to debate the issue with social scientists, felt obliged to debate it when physicist Percy Bridgman, the originator of "operationalism" as a philosophy of science and a Harvard luminary, was induced by graduate students to "debate" Stouffer on the subject at a Graduate Forum meeting in April 1948. Bridgman's contribution was to observe that the meaningful use of mathematics in the social sciences would require "the ability to analyze and describe significantly," and he went on to explain that

> significant description is the ability to pick out features of the situation which cohere together and around which you can build a theory. Significant description and theory go hand in hand. You can't have one without the other. They are a mutual growth. (SAS, p. 6)

This was not a welcome message either to Stouffer, who replied with a defense of progress in measurement and his medical model of the development of sociology, or to Parsons, who at this time was working on the collaborative project that led to *Toward a General Theory of Action* (a project lavishly funded by the Carnegie Corporation, which had also given a large unrestricted grant to the Department of Social Relations' research program).

The various programmatic statements written during the period differ from one another in various ways. Stouffer's formulations were, if not the most influential, of the best articulation of the conventional views of the dominant, quantitatively oriented segment of the community around the SSRC and the foundations. The purposes of social science were conceived in terms of an analogy with medicine as well:

> For a century after Newton the students of diseases were beguiled by the search for a great principle of disease which

would be medicine's theory of gravitation. Dr. Benjamin
Rush of Philadelphia thought he had it, a century and a half
ago, in his theory of convulsive action. We now know, of
course, that not one grand conceptual scheme, but many
limited generalizations were to mark the conquest of many
of mankind's scourges. Germ theories were useful for certain diseases, deficiency theories for others, psychosomatic
theories for yet others. Some day a synthesis of these theories may be found, but the ideas of Pasteur have been rather
fruitful for research and for the saving of living in the
absence of that synthesis. (Reply to Bridgman, 1948, SAS,
p. 6)

Stouffer did not abandon the notion of a theoretical social
science. Indeed, he formulated it in a terminology that owed
much to the logical positivists who were then making their
presence felt in American universities and who proposed a model
of the future of social science that was a sharp departure from
Pearsonian skepticism about "theory" that had governed the
programmatic and methodological writings of the earlier generation of empiricist sociologists. "We have faith," he wrote to
Harvard President James Bryant Conant,

> that there can be developed in the social sciences a body of
> theory, operationally formulated and empirically tested,
> from which predictions can be made about what will hap-
> pen in practical situations. We conceive of social science
> neither as a collection of facts, nor as a melange of common
> sense ideas and intrinsically untestable hypotheses, nor as
> a collection of research gadgets. (October 25, 1947, SAS)

The emphasis on "practical situations" was qualified in a
specific way. Many of the successes of statistical method in the
social realm, including his own organization, "involved essentially the sophisticated application of common sense, not scientific theory, to practical problems" (Stouffer, Letter to Conant,
October 25, 1947, SAS). Stouffer aspired to something more and
believed that he had achieved something more in the postwar

analyses of his wartime data on the American soldier—for example, his counterintuitive results on "relative deprivation."

These formulations differentiated him from his colleague, Talcott Parsons, whose programmatic statements focused on the necessity for conceptual integration.[11] Parsons was himself commissioned by the SSRC to write a programmatic statement for the social sciences as a whole, for the purpose of explaining the prospects of social science and justifying the claim of social science to public support. The draft of this document, which was unacceptable to the committee that commissioned it and never used, is a good example of the new genre, although Parsons wrote many others during this period. Indeed, virtually the whole body of Parsons's work in his extraordinarily productive period from 1943 to 1953 consisted of efforts to lay out a comprehensive theoretical strategy and to provide preliminary analyses that showed the potential fruitfulness of the strategy. Some of these writings, such as "The Position of Sociological Theory" (1948), were published; others such as his "Common Language for the Social Sciences" proposal were not, but were nonetheless influential in constituting the Department of Social Relations and the Social Relations Laboratory—the administrative structures Parsons used to further his ideas. The significance of these statements goes beyond their value as indications of Parsons's theoretical intentions; they were serious attempts to influence powerful audiences, such as the Harvard hierarchy and funding sources, to act in terms of a particular vision of social science and to accept the new standards of worthiness entailed by this vision.

Parsons later would characterize Merton's variant program of concentrating on "theories of the middle range," introduced at the 1948 ASS meetings, as a relatively benign competitor to his own and would suggest that "in retrospect" it seems to have been "a very constructive move that was necessary to integrate the empirical with the theoretical" (1968, p. ix). Merton did not, of course, deal with Parsons directly or critically in this statement, much less mount a philosophical assault on his premises; rather, he stayed within the bounds of the programmatic genre. Yet the intended effect of the statement was similar to that of a methodological polemic. It served to provide an alternative standard for evaluation of the cognitive validity of present efforts at research and theory. These were not, however, consensual beliefs in either the community of elite researchers or in the discipline at large. Lazarsfeld, for example, considered empirical research and theory to be, in effect, two distinct disciplines; and many of the demographically oriented methodologists saw no relevance to theory in any form.

THE SURVEY PARADIGM:
THE NEW MODEL RESEARCH
PROJECT AND ITS CONSEQUENCES

In a sense, the level of quantitative sophistication of the new surveys, especially the tactic that Lazarsfeld had imported from market research, and the construction of psychological indices based on questionnaires were duplicatable activities, and indeed they were endlessly duplicated. As a result of the technical advance in sampling theory described in the last chapter, it now became possible to perform inexpensive small surveys and analyses of bodies of existing data. The next step was the introduction of the practice of significance testing. Oddly enough, one of the first examples of this in sociology was in an article published by Merton in the *American Sociological Review* (*ASR*) in 1947, but the practice only slowly gained acceptance. No such tests are found in *The American Soldier* (Stouffer et al., 1949); the BASR publications through the 1950s generally avoided them even where sampling considerations justified their use; and the students of the Bureau polemicized against them (see Lipset, Trow, and Coleman, 1962).

Nevertheless, the practice spread very quickly among quantitatively oriented sociologists outside of the circles around Lazarsfeld and Stouffer. Those who adopted significance tests were perhaps influenced more by local connections to statisticians in other fields—for example, agricultural statistics, psychology, and the departments of statistics that were being established during this period at several of the major state universities. The ease with which one could calculate the "level of significance" of results led to a kind of inversion of past ways of thinking about the problem of inferences from a particular finding, making it even easier to produce "significant" results from small samples. Instead of thinking of the "confidence interval" around a finding as an expression of the limitation of one's predictive powers, the strength of a confident finding of a difference itself became a kind of separate fact, a test of "having a result," which could then be replicated for other populations and circumstances. What was learned, very quickly, was that "significant" results could be produced easily with small samples and that new "hypotheses" using "measures" of "variables," such as anomie, could be easily concocted. In many cases these measures had some tenuous connection to the theoretical tradition of sociology,[12] though in many cases the research simply served to find significant relationships between some outcome of interest and standard demographic categorizations.

The typical study done under this model was a dissertation or journal article that had the following form: a review of the "theory" behind the problem (usually no more than a few remarks on the interest of a past master in some more or less closely related problem, and at times no more than a reference to the previous research on the subject); a formulation of a "hypothesis" and discussion of the sample, the "design" of the research, and the methods of measurement or operationalizing the "concepts"; the presentation of findings, usually presented in tables and accompanied by a discussion of the statistical methods that produced a judgment of significance; and a conclusion that suggested some researchable implications of the finding.

The "hypothesis" had a novel form. The controversial innovation in the statistical theory of the 1930s was the idea of "acceptance," particularly the idea that a measure of significance could be regarded as a measure of the cognitive acceptability of certain kinds of inferences,[13] typically taking the form of a "null" hypothesis of no difference or no relationship, which the research was designed to test, and which would, if rejected, warrant the acceptance of a hypothesis of difference. The difficulty with this account was that it confused, or encouraged confusion over, the relationship between "substantive" and "statistical" significance. The basis for this confusion was laid in the 1930s with the idea, formulated by Stouffer in 1934, that the inferences of interest were to a hypothetical "universe" rather than merely to the empirically existing population as a whole.[14]

The spread of this new research format was dramatic. An enormous number of quantitative studies of this kind were produced, and in a few years, the number of "findings" and relationships, as well as new "measures" and topics newly colonized by sociology through the demonstration that some aggregate pattern, such as the consumption of particular kinds of health service, was significantly related to some "social" variable, such as occupational status. By 1965, no less than 2500 "measures" had been invented and reported in the sociological literature, and an enormous body of methodological folklore had grown up about the pitfalls of various methods, samples, and statistical techniques for assessing hypotheses.

The historical relation between this new "standard sociology" and the kind of large-scale survey sociology performed under the influence of Lazarsfeld and Stouffer is puzzling. Many of the participants in the research performed by Stouffer during the war were midwesterners and returned to the universities of the Midwest as sociologists. Arnold Rose, for example, spent his career at Minnesota, one of the dominant departments of the Midwest, which placed most of its many graduates in lesser universities in the region. The students of Lazarsfeld were not so widely distributed. Some of the sociologists who had been employed in large-scale survey work for the BASR, ISR, or NORC during the 1950s were able to secure appointments in the sociology departments at these or other elite universities, but for the most part they did not gain appointments to the large midwestern departments that were numerically dominant during this period. Moreover, the models of research established by the BASR and the foundation grants were not readily adapted to the conditions of academic life in these departments. Lone scholarship and small-scale quantitative research that could be done with the help of a few graduate student assistants working on dissertations was the norm for these departments and numerically dominated the profession as a whole.

Little of this work was directly inspired by Lazarsfeld or Stouffer. "Reasons analysis" was used only by Lazarsfeld's own students, and the distinctive measurement idea of Lazarsfeld, "latent structure analysis," also found few users. The new measures were for the most part of the more mundane variety pioneered by Chapin and his students. The statistical methods used were very diverse: factor analysis; nonparametric methods, such as chi-square; and correlation analysis can all be found in this period. For the ordinary sociologist, then, the importance of the large well-funded surveys was primarily to be found in the prestige they bestowed on quantification. Small-scale research developed on its own terms with the expansion of university enrollments. The gradual change in university expectations for research made it necessary for these sociologists to publish articles, and these methods provided a simple solution to the problems of cost and organization that plagued organizations like the BASR.

The worm in this apple was success itself. Not only was this new mode of research easily taught and performed, it was so easily done that the kinds of clear "results" that early research of this kind had produced were often clouded by later research that showed differences within the differences, plausible alternatives, and differences between subpopulations with respect to the differences.

One consequence of the proliferations of findings and their lack of relation to the tradition as taught in theory courses was the problem of "theory" and research. The expansion of methodological folklore and the creation of elaborate divisions of labor within the ranks of the researchers meant that, for the first time in the history of the discipline, researchers of the quantitative sort typically knew little "theory" and had few "theoretical" ambitions. In contrast to Ogburn and Chapin, each of whom had elaborate theoretical ideas about cultural change, the new methodologists had no loyalty to the canonical problems and were often trained by persons who had no special knowledge of the sociological literature—Lazarsfeld and Goodman were conspicuous examples, but not the only ones. Bernard Berelson, for example, was a library scientist by training.

THEORY AND RESEARCH

The discrepancy between theory and research took several forms. In the case of many students trained in the large survey research shops, the pattern was that they received virtually no exposure to any theoretical literature; instead, they were trained primarily to perform specialized technical tasks in the elaborate divisions of labor that had developed in these shops. In the programs at Columbia and Harvard, they were taught the views of Parsons and Merton as well as the distinctive Parsonian conception of the European tradition. But the prior American tradition was not a part of either thinker's theoretical *weltanschauung*. At Chicago, the local tradition survived in the teachings of Herbert Blumer, but when Blumer left to establish the department of sociology at the University of California, Berkeley, and when Everett C. Hughes departed, even this small dose of the old tradition ceased. In the rest of American sociology, theory continued to be taught, though in a less restrictive manner. For example, in the 1920s Chapin taught a survey of a great many thinkers, and this more ecumenical style of theory teaching continued in the divergent versions of the European tradition propounded by Howard P. Becker at Wisconsin, and, later, Don Martindale at Minnesota.

Although Parsons and Merton represented new blood and new ideas, they were received by these audiences as having responded to problems already salient within the sociological community. As we have suggested, the widely endorsed aspirations of Eubank for a synthetic integration of "the concepts of sociology" were heralds of Parsons's efforts. The "functionalism" of Merton and the various other Harvard students of the 1930s, such as Kingsley Davis and Robin Williams, was even more readily accepted. The reasons for this may be readily understood. Consider the following paradigmatically "functionalist" passage:

> This essay is an attempt to interpret education in the light of one of its principal social functions. By education is meant the training of younger generations by the older members of the community. The adults may instruct in their capacity as parents, as participants in ceremony, or as members of a civil institution. In any of these cases their activities have the support of social sanction. This sanction is group approval, expressed or implied, of any activity which is conducive to group welfare or survival. Since group success is generally associated with certain traditions, to conserve them becomes the aim of education. (Chapin, 1911, p. 5).

This level of generality, the stress on group sanctions and the reproduction and conservation of sanctioned "traditions," and the appeal to group success or survival as the ultimate ground of explanation are characteristic of the functionalism that developed at Harvard in the 1930s and 1940s. But this passage is the opening paragraph of Stuart Chapin's dissertation of 1911 at Columbia.

The deep similarities are not accidental, for the language of functionalism, such as the paired terms *structure and function*, is simply the language of the Spencerianism that had been central to Giddings and Sumner and important for virtually every early American sociologist. This same Spencerianism had also infused itself into the empirical research traditions of the earlier generations of American sociologists, for the problem of the "functioning" of community institutions was precisely the issue around which much of the "social survey" research of the past had been conceived. Indeed, this patronage vehicle had been structured by the idea, shared by the researchers and the community leaders who supported the surveys, of "efficiency," an idea that was understood in terms of the goals of the community. Parsons's

"Hobbesian problem of order" was another form of the familiar problem of cooperation and its difficulties. Giddings and his students were as much a part of the "explicit revolt against the traditions of economic individualism and socialism" as was Parsons in his revision of Durkheim and Weber and as Durkheim and Weber themselves were.

Parsons's work, and the more straightforward "functionalist" work of the Harvard students of the 1930s and 1940s, such as Davis and Moore (1945), was thus not read as a radical departure, but rather as a reaffirmation of what American theory had always possessed. This in part explains the puzzling reception of Parsons's works. For in spite of the localized Harvard inspirations of the work, notably the Paretianism of the L. J. Henderson circle, Parsonianism was readily assimilated into the dominant currents of the time. What his critics rejected was not his model of humans or of his sociology but his special jargon and his peculiar metatheoretical ideas. Sociologists in the Midwest were comfortable paying homage to Parsons, while in practice ignoring him entirely because they believed that his account added nothing of substance to what they already had, except perhaps in providing the legitimating *mana* of the great European sociologists.

Parsons did add to the ambient structural functionalism in what he later called his " 'structural-functional' phase" (1968, p. xii). One difference was the reorganization of the idea of function through the introduction of the Pareto/Henderson/Cannon (Cross and Albury, 1987)/Radcliffe-Brown notion of "system," which was quite definitely not part of the ambient structural functionalism, and the systematic reintroduction of explicit teleological reasoning. But these additions were the most controversial element of Parsonianism, and the most heavily criticized. What is perhaps more significant is what Parsons left out of the received "theoretical" tradition, the kind of theory writing he and Merton delegitimated, and the accommodation they made to "empirical" sociology.

By the late 1920s, as we have seen, some quantitative sociologists were quite ready to drum theory out of the discipline. But in the wake of Ellwood's failed revolt against scientism—which left a permanent minority hostile to the dominant ideals and largely excluded from the ASS and the major journals—the younger sociologists who were still in the elite made their separate and sometimes idiosyncratic accommodations with the scientistic ideal. Blumer's writings of the 1930s, under the political protection of the powerful Ellsworth Faris, but in a department closely allied to the SSRC model of social science and the SRA elite, insisted on "control" as the criterion of a good scientific theory in his critique of Thomas and Znaniecki (1939). Parsons's accommodation was even more idiosyncratic, for it appears superficially to be something other than an accommodation, being rather a new enterprise opposed to empiricism. In fact, as his defenders have recently argued (Lidz, 1986), that was far from his intent. Although Mills's (1959) characterization of Parsons at the end of this period as a "Grand Theorist" has stuck, and Parsons described himself as an "incurable theorist," he nevertheless held a view of the relation between theory and research that was considerably more accommodating to empirical research than many of the earlier "theorists" had been. To understand Parsons's work in the context of the intradisciplinary divisions of the time, it is necessary to reexamine the reception of Parsons's work, and notice the character of his and Merton's distinctions between the kind of theoretical writing they themselves were doing and that of their older contemporaries.

When the *ASR* was established in the mid-1930s, one of the domains for which it was explicitly responsible was "the history of social thought," by which was meant the study of past social thinkers—a traditional topic in sociology curricula from the beginning of the discipline and the academic specialization of many of its members, such as Ellwood, Floyd House, Howard P. Becker, and Harry Elmer Barnes. As the case of Ellwood suggests, these writers tended to see the history of social thought as a series of failed doctrines or systems, which contained lessons about social reasoning that could be applied to present vernacular social thinking and to attempts at "scientific" social theory. Most of these writers were, in a loose sense, philosophical pragmatists who saw the process of correcting and improving ideas as open and continuous, without an aim at a fixed and monistic end point. The age of the systems, they thought, had passed, but the systems of the past were inevitably the starting point for attempts at understanding the present. They drew no sharp line between scientific and vernacular social thinking, and the Roosevelt era, with its many ideological quandaries over the relation between the public and private realms and the role of rational state planning, seemed to validate the importance of the tradition that they expounded. In Ellwood's terms, it was the political embodiment of the dispute between Sumner and Ward (Ellwood, 1938).

The effect of Parsons's *The Structure of Social Action* (1968), with its hypothesis of a hidden shared conceptual system underlying the contributions of the main "scientific" theorists of social action, and the distinction made by Merton in his article of 1948 on the history and systematics of sociological was to redefine the purpose of theoretical writing, its audience, and the aim of theory. They were not philosophical pragmatists compelled to ask the questions of the felt needs to which the theories of the past were responses; they were comfortable in regarding whole ranges of past social thought as pointless and erroneous drivel and dismissing them accordingly. The contrast between this attitude and such texts as Barnes's and Becker's *Social Thought from Lore to Science* (1938) and Barnes's *An Introduction to the History of Sociology* (1948) could not be more striking. Parsons's aim was to extract the elements of past theory relevant to his systematic project, a project which he conceived in a fashion that would not be antagonistic to the claims of empirical sociology properly understood. He had little interest in the audience that Barnes and Ellwood regarded as central, the politically conscious public with a felt need for the clarification and revision of their own social ideas, though he was well aware of its presence and of the demand for the sociologists' contribution.

Barnes in particular honored no *disciplinary* boundaries; like other products of the Columbia degree program, which was still called "Social Science" until 1940, he spoke as a member of various disciplines and stressed the interrelations of the social sciences (Ogburn and Goldenweiser, 1927; cf. also Barnes, 1925;

Beard, 1934). Similarly, Ellwood was deeply influenced by anthropological writers on cultural evolution, and he incorporated
their ideas into his own sociological writings. Parsons offered
something different, and it was evidently part of his appeal to
graduate students in the 1930s and later. He argued, in response
to his own situation at Harvard where the social sciences were
dominated by a powerful economics department, that there was
a special domain for sociology not shared by any other theoretical
discipline (Levine, 1980, p. xi; Camic, 1979). Thus his work served
as a means of identity-formation for students, and his account of
the prehistory of the problems served as a source of pride for
those who shared these aims (Heeren, 1975).

The mismatch between the older idea of the history of social
thought, with its critical tone, and the new statistical scientism,
with its deep desire to make sociology into a science like the
natural sciences, became evident only gradually. In the 1930s,
writers like Chapin could serenely identify themselves as "theorists" and addressed the theoretical problem of the day, cultural
change, without sensing any deep conflict with their methodological views. Their theories were informal and corresponded
to the rough correlations that could be discerned in the empirical
world by the researcher in possession of the appropriate statistical techniques. The idea of the possibility of radical improvement
in precision in measurement changed this situation irrevocably.
The consequence for theory, as seen by the methodologists, was
this: theory was to serve as a means of clarifying the domains to
be rendered precise and was to be a source of hypotheses (of
limited generality, in Stouffer's "medical" formulation) that
could be made more precise and tested. The *ideal* form of theory,
then, had to match the goal of precision, and theories that could
not be seen as steps toward this goal were therefore scientifically
irrelevant. Stouffer's formulation of the ideal is quite explicit:
interrelated propositions that can be put in the form, "If $x1$, given
$x2$ and $x3$, then there is a strong probability that we get $x4$."
Parsons, it will be observed, embraced this standard, or something similar, in his 1948 paper "The Prospects of Sociological
Theory," and assigned himself the task of conceptual clarification

of the domain through an elaborated theoretical scheme. Stouffer did not accept the necessity for a scheme of precisely this kind, but he agreed that the existence of some "more general scheme of things" was essential to progress. Without it, sociology would be confined to being a "fact-finding" enterprise; with it, sociology could construct something analogous to crucial experiments, where the consequences of the results for other hypotheses can be determined (Stouffer, 1950, p. 359). The enterprise of Parsonian theory and the tactic of improved precision would thus be reconciled. The older kind of theory could not be reconciled.

This new model of the purpose of theory implied the elimination of the older category of "history of social thought" from the standard descriptions of the division of labor in sociology; indeed, this category of theory is nowhere to be found in such texts as Parsons's (1986) SSRC proposal, Donald Young's (1948) characterization of the problems and needs of the social sciences, or Stouffer's (1950) explications of the proximate aims of sociology. In fact, there was active hostility, which found political expression in such reforms as the demand for "administrative discrimination between publications which gives greater weight to scientific articles than to learned essays, descriptive reports, syntheses in the nature of textbooks," and popularizations (Young, 1948, p. 332) (i.e., the main literary vehicles of the older history of social thought).[15]

These strategies were successful. One indication of this is the decline in the number of sociologists who identified themselves as historians of social thought, which became a category in which it was difficult to find employment despite the general expansion of the field.[16] Articles of the old type were not easy to publish in the "scientific" journals, and many of the authors who wished to study theory in the old way found it difficult to survive in the new academic environment. In the most prestigious departments, with the greatest access to time, resources, and good graduate students, none of them did, though several were to be found at second-tier universities.

The process by which the history of social thought was driven underground was paralleled in a broad sense throughout the field. Many of the sociologists who were not part of the community of foundation-funded researchers in the immediate postwar period were insulated from the constraining effects of these relationships, and, as a result, they simply continued to do what they considered to be "normal sociology" in a tradition to which they believed themselves to have an equal or greater right than the nonsociologists at Harvard and Columbia. The continuities at such universities as Minnesota and Washington were strong, and the sense of possession of the sociological tradition that characterized the training of sociologists in these departments owed little to Parsons, Stouffer, Lazarsfeld, or Merton. These departments continued earlier developments toward small statistical research projects and the creation of loose ad hoc measures of individual, rather than community, properties. Yet, for the most part, these developments were not in direct conflict with large-scale survey work, and the lines between the styles of work grew indistinct as the emphases of Lazarsfeld and Stouffer faded in the 1940s.

The easy adoption of such persons as Goodman and Lazarsfeld was not simply a reflection of a lack of development in sociology; the employment of these persons served particular purposes for the departments and networks that adopted them. The relentless propagandizing for the scientific method and the identification of science with metricization that had occupied the generation of George Lundberg and Read Bain was a necessary preliminary for the acceptance of survey research as the paradigmatic method of sociology and the acceptance of the kinds of results that were produced by large survey projects, such as Stouffer's *The American Soldier*.

By the end of this period, new divisions arose. Many American sociologists were convinced neither by the apologetics nor the results of the research of the large survey organizations. And many more were unimpressed by the Parsonian program. In the late 1950s, several works appeared that formulated these attitudes in an aggressive fashion. Of these, the most famous were Dahrendorf's essay on Parsons, "Out of Utopia," published in 1958 (1968), which captured many Americans' sense of the pointlessness of the Parsonian enterprise, and perhaps fed on their resentment of Parson's academic standing and the power of the Ivy League/foundation community. More important was the book by C. Wright Mills, *The Sociological Imagination* (1959). As a Wisconsin Ph.D. with many personal connections to the hinter-land,[17] Mills was a natural antagonist to Parsons, Merton, Lazars-feld, and the academic class system that they represented. The book, which concealed under its abstract headings an ethno-graphically precise characterization of the Columbian scene and, in particular, the BASR, was a reaffirmation of the intellectual values that Donald Young disdained, especially the value that Mills called "intellectual craftsmanship." The title *The Sociological Imagination* itself evoked the strong tacit sense of the sociological perspective that had developed in the departments of the Mid-west by the 1970s, which the theoretical and technical concerns of Parsons, Merton, and Lazarsfeld never matched.

The argument of the text shows both its roots in the older American sociological tradition and its deviation from it. Mills begins by considering the felt intellectual needs of the day and shows why sociology is failing to meet them. The proper role of social science in society is precisely to make reason relevant to democracy and to be a part of public discourse, even if this consisted only in challenging "official definitions of reality" (Mills, 1959, p. 191). What he rejected was the older individualis-tic bias of such reformist sociologists as John Gillin. In its place he urged an institutional comparative historical approach inte-grated with an understanding of the relationship between larger social structures and personality and motivated not by models of "science" but by "a sense of real problems as they arise out of history" (p. 72). On the level of method, he called for pluralism, and did not challenge the methods of empirical sociology as methods. But he suggested that methodology could not be based on the philosophy of science. The then fashionable logical posi-tivism was perceived to be in a kind of alliance with conventional survey methodology and functionalism.[18] Mills argued, against it, that advance in methods is "most likely to occur as modest generalizations stemming from work in progress" (p. 122).

There is a curious symmetry between Mills's assessment and that made by Parsons at the same moment. Both grasped that the 1960s would be the decade of sociology, and both saw that the university was a potential battleground. For Mills, it was the venue of necessity in the absence of appropriate "democratic parties and movements" (1959, p. 191). The profession had already become divided over the problem of sociology's relation to the social problems of the day. The rural sociologists had established a separate society in the 1930s. In the 1950s, the Society for the Study of Social Problems was created in response to the sense of many sociologists that the "professionalization" of the ASS, recently renamed the American Sociological Association (ASA), amounted to an abandonment of the discipline's traditional concerns with the poor and powerless. For Parsons, serving as chairman of the Committee on the Profession of the ASA, it was a problem "confronting sociology as a profession," falling under the heading of the relationship between sociology and "the nonscientific aspects of the general culture." This problem was, in turn, compounded by others: the problem of the discipline itself "as a cultural complex" and, particularly, the problem of "the extent to which the canons of scientific adequacy and objectivity have come to be established as the working code of the profession" (Parsons, 1959, p. 547). Two dilemmas arose from this compound problem. The first concerned the demand for sociology, particularly at the undergraduate level, which was then "primarily a general education function, helping to prepare the student for the world in which he lives" (p. 554). At the time, Parsons claimed, this was itself colored by a broad ideological preoccupation with the problem of conformity, the theme of his Harvard peer David Riesman (1950). But the public would potentially define the sociologist as an "expert" in these kinds of issues, and Parsons saw this as an opportunity for sociology to seize center stage in the public eye, as economics had earlier.

This "ideological" concern of the public and of undergraduate students, Parsons felt, had replaced the earlier, simpler concern with "social evils" and it imposes a heavy responsibility on sociologists. An ideology is precisely a meeting ground between a society's value commitments and its empirical scientific culture. In the nature of the case powerful pressures come into conflict with standards of scientific objectivity. (1959, p. 555)

To the "purists" who counsel "withdrawal" in the face of this situation, "by avoiding all connection with this wider forum of discussion," he observed that this is feasible only for "certain purely technical specialists. For the profession as a whole, it is an impossible position to take" (p. 555). As his readers were well aware, to turn away these students would be to cut the ground from under the claim of sociology to the resources of the university.

Parsons's solution to the problem of demand for expertise was to develop the "applied" side of sociology more adequately, perhaps through an expansion of the use of "the consultant role in various nonacademic organizations," and the increased presence of sociologists in the professional schools. Both trends were developing at the time and were accompanied by the creation of centers for "action research," but it was necessary to insist on the highest professional standards in training (1959, p. 557).

CONCLUSION

The period after World War II—roughly between 1946 and 1960—set the stage for sociology's "Golden Era." It was a transitional period, marked by the emergence of new intellectual leaders, new levels of funding, new sources of funding, renewed student interest in sociology (after the sharp drop in demand in the mid-1950s), and renewed efforts to reconcile theory, methods, and practice.

The new leaders were the result of professional demography, as the generation of Ph.D.'s trained before World War I died and retired, creating vacancies that the sporadic production of Ph.D.'s during the Depression could not fill. Moreover, new positions were being created as the colleges of the old Ivy League began to assert themselves as research-oriented universities.

The material base for this resurgence was a renewed wave of funding by private foundations, but the old networks of foundation officers and selected academics were about to recede in the face of dramatic increases in federal funding of academic research. The beginnings of this transition, involving public monies and peer review, were clearly evident in the 1950s.

The emergence of quantitative social psychology and functional theorizing were the great intellectual achievements of this period. The emphasis on measurement and quantitative statistical analysis had been building for many decades, gradually pushing alternative approaches to the margins. Yet this ascendancy appeared to be, at least for a time, a "bloodless" coup, as the incidence of methodological polemics was not great. Even more surprising was the apparent accommodation between functional theory and the new emphasis on quantitative methods—an accommodation greatly facilitated by the Parsons-Stouffer and Merton-Lazarsfeld connections at Harvard and Columbia, respectively. There were, however, faint rumblings about the relation of theory and practice, the problems of functional theory, and the overemphasis on quantitative methods. Yet these issues were not to become polarizing into the 1960s and 1970s. In fact, theorists such as Parsons argued in favor of sociology developing its applied side in professional schools and in using the tools of theory and research to extend sociology's influence.

Organizationally, sociology began to grow. The number of degrees awarded fluctuated, but was on the rise as the 1960s approached—providing an important resource for faculty job creation. And ASA membership increased dramatically amidst rumblings about making sociology a bigger, more powerful, and more coherent professional organization. Such aspirations, however, were to be overwhelmed by the massive influx of resources in the next decade which, in a sense, caused such rapid growth and differentiation that intellectual integration and organizational coherence became impossible. The points of potential tension among theory, methods, practice, and critique were all to resurface as each gathered new resources, and the emergence of new subfields, journals, and specialty associations was to accelerate to inconceivable proportions in the next decades.

The kinds of historical events outlined in Chapters 1-3 were soon to be overwhelmed by the influx of new resources. The avalanche of money and students allowed sociology to grow and differentiate to such an extent that the details of particular persons and events—more critical, perhaps, when resources are limited—became less compelling than the sheer volume and magnitude of increases in material resources, particularly students and research funds. Intellectually and organizationally, American sociology was not prepared for or able to pull together the new differentiation of the field—as our history of sociology up to this present period would clearly suggest. From its beginnings, American sociology has consisted of uneasy compromises among potentially conflicting aspirations, views, and organizational forms. But what happens when resources increase to the point where the need to compromise or pull together is greatly reduced because there is something for all? Such is the story of the next chapter.

NOTES

1. MacIver, himself a nonsociologist who had been made chairman at Columbia after Giddings's departure from the scene, was an insider at Columbia, trusted by the hierarchy and by the New York philanthropists for whom he performed many "evaluations" of projects. He was on cordial but not close terms with the methodological dissidents, such as Sorokin and Ellwood, and his *Social Causation* (1942) was a contribution to the literature critical of the philosophy of science behind conventional sociological methodology, and particularly the Pearsonianism of Giddings and his followers.

2. MacIver was a foreigner, as was, of course, Sorokin. Theodore Abel was a Pole. Merton, a Jew, cultivated the image of urbanity that these faculties demanded.

3. See Converse (1987). This is a C. C. Taylor story.

4. In his commentary on Parsons's draft of an SSRC appeal in the postwar period, Samuel Klausner remarks on the mystical importance the academic leaders of the SSRC imputed to "diversity" of funding sources (1986, p. 5). In view of their experience with the Rockefeller almoners, this is hardly surprising, and they were right about the liberating effect of the diversity that followed.

Parsons, it may be noted, did not hold such pluralistic views, as Klausner points out.

5. Vance Packard's (1957) book, *The Hidden Persuaders*, which gave one of Lazarsfeld's wives, Herta Herzog, as an example, popularized the motivational research business. By the 1960s, these efforts had become the subject of endless satirization and the motivational psychologist a comic type, as in such films as *Putney Swope*.

6. Lazarsfeld himself freely discussed the resource problems that he faced at different periods and the advantages of various solutions to them (in PFLW for example).

7. This research was conducted as a small part of the work of an organization primarily concerned with physical and economic damage, but it involved an exceptional interdisciplinary group of social scientists, including the political scientists David Truman and William Sewell, as well as psychologists, sampling specialists, anthropologists, and others. They determined that increased bombing had little effect on morale in Germany and little differential effect in Japan between heavily bombed and untouched regions (cf. Sewell, 1988; Converse, 1987, pp. 174-180).

8. Stouffer and Lazarsfeld each spent a great deal of time explaining away the various failures of polling, especially after the fiasco of the 1948 presidential election predictions. Stouffer's strategy, however, was to sharply distinguish survey research from polling.

9. Compare Stouffer to Speier (1949) in SAS. Significant Rockefeller support of this kind of work was given through a joint NRC/SSRC Committee chaired by Stouffer in 1945 (Converse, 1986, p. 229).

10. The failure of the BASR and other survey research units with academic pretensions to solve the problem of compromises with clients' demands was strongly felt by many of the participants in this research. The conflicts were less severe in the relatively few cases where foundation officers and academics agreed on an agenda for sociology and on the importance of various problems and methods. Thus the products of this period and these grants were pinnacles of achievements that later studies found difficult to reach, even when funding was more generous, for they were addressed to an increasingly divided academic audience concerned either with issues arising internally within the expanding discipline or with topics of limited significance.

11. This was a respectable idea in SSRC circles as well (cf. Young, 1948, p. 330).

12. Philippe Besnard has written about the transformation of the concept of anomie by Srole in these terms, making the important point that the concept had little or no connection to Durkheim's use, but served certain polemical purposes in the debate over the relation between theory and research (1987, pp. 223-284; 1986).

13. The key document was Neyman's paper "On the Two Different Aspects of the Representative Method" (1934).

14. In the 1950s, the whole subject of "significance" produced an enormous and obscure literature attempting to disentangle the two sides of the concept. The problem that this literature tended to overlook was that the test itself was extremely weak, simply because the null hypotheses whose rejection was at

issue were in fact usually known to be literally false or highly improbable (Meehl, 1967).

15. The expansion of opportunities for the publication of nontextbook material was considered an important achievement of the period. Parsons, commenting on these developments, singled out his own publisher, The Free Press, for its importance in demonstrating the existence of a market for "serious nontextbook publications in sociology" to other publishing houses (1959, p. 557). The virtual collapse of this house, and the withdrawal from the market of many other houses in the early 1970s is indicative of the contraction of this market.

16. Many persons with these interests changed their label to "social change," and the increase in this category is in part a reflection of this fact (cf. Zetterberg, 1956).

17. Despite the high ranking of departments like Wisconsin, Minnesota, and North Carolina in this period, very few of the graduates of these universities were ever appointed in the Ivy League. C. Wright Mills was an apparent exception and was therefore something of a hero to the sociologists of the hinterland, but he was appointed only in the undergraduate unit of Columbia and excluded from the graduate program.

18. The appearance of a close relation between the two was enhanced by the contribution of a paper giving an analysis of functional explanation to a volume on sociological theory (Gross, 1959) and by the writings of such persons as Hans Zetterberg, a Swedish sociologist with connections to Lazarsfeld, who actually taught a seminar with Ernest Nagel at Columbia. Most of the connections were superficial, however, including Lazarsfeld's own. In the few cases where analytic philosophers of any kind discussed actual sociological theory or explanation, the results were quite critical (e.g., Black, 1961). Many of the quantitative sociologists liked the positivist message, especially the suggestion that explanations and theory in all sciences take the same basic logical form. The drive within positivism to assimilate extant forms of scientific practice, then, served to legitimate their scientific pretensions, and, incidentally, to underline the importance of theory, a theme of importance to 1950s positivism that had not been part of the Machian prehistory of positivism. The apparent alliance, however, shaped the debates of the 1960s and 1970s, as critiques of conventional philosophy of science were deployed against conventional sociological methodology, as was the philosophical literature concerned with distinguishing explanations in physical domains and the domain of human action, of which Winch (1958) was the most famous example.

FOUR

The "Golden Era" and Its Aftermath: American Sociology Today

THE INCREASE IN RESOURCES

When the Soviet Union launched its Sputnik satellite into orbit on October 4, 1957, the presumed superiority of American technology was suddenly questionable—at least in a symbolic sort of way. The years that followed witnessed a dramatic effort to restructure the American educational system in order to assure that there would be enough scientists and technical personnel to meet this new challenge. The National Defense Education Act, which was passed after considerable haggling, debate, compromise, and redirection, created the vehicle by which massive amounts of money were to be transferred from the government to higher education (Clowse, 1981). Subsequent additions, amendments, and augmentations to this act over the next decade expanded physical facilities of colleges and universities as well as the ability of undergraduate and graduate students to finance their education. Moreover, federal agencies experienced dramatic increases in funds that they could pass on to students, faculties, and university research facilities.

While the "hard sciences" profited most from these benefits, the social sciences also received a significant increase in their level of support. The end result was for the nature of funding for the social sciences in general and sociology in particular to move decisively away from private foundations to public agencies, primarily in the federal government. For example, between 1956 and 1980, the money to the social sciences from private foundations doubled (from $21 million to $41 million, a decrease in constant dollars), but the monies from the federal government increased 17 times over (from $30 million in 1956 to $424 million in 1980). These funds were coupled with a 27-fold increase in monies from the universities to researchers (most of this also coming indirectly from the federal government), so that a large supply of funds for new physical facilities, faculty development, student support through loans and fellowships, and faculty research was now available. In addition, a growing market outside of academia for "contract research" financed both by private firms and public agencies was emerging. Figures 4.1, 4.2, 4.3, and 4.4 give a rough sense of the increased level of federal funding of sociology in the post-Sputnik era.

The various forces increasing the scale of sociology during the 1960s are not easily disentangled, but the effects of funding are crucial. Expanded funding increased the number of graduate students; as Figures 4.5 and 4.6 document, the number of Ph.D.'s and M.A.'s granted annually in sociology rose very quickly. These graduate enrollments provided sociology with a demographic resource that could be used to expand graduate programs. Previously, as Figure 3.2 documented, Ph.D. production had fluctuated throughout the 1950s after a general overexpansion in the immediate postwar period, which had left many well-trained academics at nonresearch institutions—small liberal arts colleges, teachers colleges, low-prestige state schools, and community colleges. The attractiveness of an academic career in sociology had thus decreased in the pre-Sputnik period, and, coupled with declining college enrollments in the 1950s (as the backlog of Korean War veterans disappeared), there was uncertainty among students about an academic career. The post-Sput-

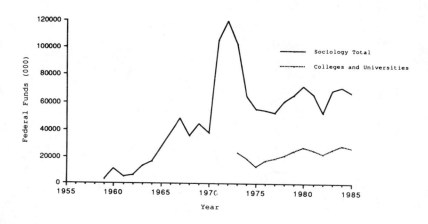

Figure 4.1. Federal Funds for Sociology: Total and Colleges and
        Universities

nik expansion of support changed all this, easing the way for
students who otherwise would not have been able to afford to
complete a Ph.D.

Undergraduate demand was also an important factor in sociology's growth. After dropping in the 1950s, the number of students enrolled in sociology began to climb, slowly but consistently. The superheating of student demand for sociology began
in 1962, just before the baby-boom generation entered the university in force in the mid- to late-1960s. Figure 4.7 documents how
dramatic the increase in student enrollments was during this
period. In addition to the demographics of the baby-boom generation there were the radicalizing effects of the war in Vietnam—
a war which, because of its intrusion into the lives of so many
American families, demanded a great deal of public discussion
and legitimation. Moreover, the rediscovery of domestic problems, especially poverty and ethnic inequalities, stimulated further debate.

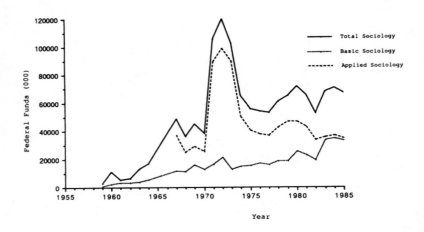

Figure 4.2. Federal Funds for All Sociology

Sociologists, and people identified by the public as "sociologists," responded to this debate by assuming a series of public roles as "explainers" of the newly problematized social world. The debate thus became a symbolic resource that sociology could use in its efforts to expand. Some sociologists became agitators, journalistic propagandists, and organizational participants in left-wing causes. For example, C. Wright Mills's two popular books of the period, *Listen, Yankee,* which was on Cuba, and *The Causes of World War III* were visible examples of a kind of sociological journalism—not unlike that which had earlier been practiced by E. A. Ross and P. A. Sorokin. Others became television personalities, such as family specialist Carlfred Broderick, who opined on problems of marriage and child rearing for the Tonight Show between such segments as magic acts and elderly starlets. Still others became spokespersons for the national "establishment," especially the group of Ivy League academics and lawyers who had made their presence felt in Washington in the Kennedy years and stayed under Johnson's presidency. Of these, Talcott Parsons himself was among the most visible, writing for such

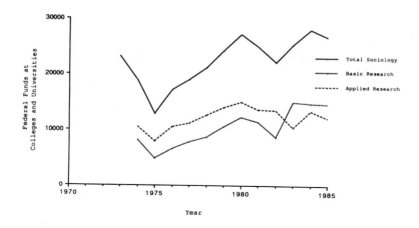

Figure 4.3. Federal Funds for Sociology at Colleges and Universities

opinion-setting journals as *Daedalus* and on the problems in various institutional sectors of American life. Irving Louis Horowitz and others established *Trans-action* (later to become *Society*), a magazine devoted to social action designed to correct the social problems described within its glossy covers.

The identity of "sociologists" in the public mind was fixed during this era, and their message was this: differences between people, whether these were differences in suicide rates or rates of coronary occlusion, crime, poverty, and the like, vary in relation to "social facts" such as class position and race; therefore, "society" is causally responsible for these differences. The moral of this story—sometimes given by the sociologist, sometimes inferred by a prepared audience—was that the state ought to intervene. The enactment of a series of government initiatives to deal with poverty, urban problems, educational reform, racial discrimination, and inequalities of opportunity had the effect on the public consciousness of identifying sociology with the promotion of these programs and, more generally, expanded government expenditure and authority. In a sense, sociology was once again dependent upon the ideological capital provided by the reformist

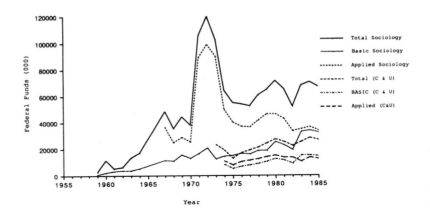

Figure 4.4. Federal Funding for Sociology: All Types

tendencies in American public opinion, but this time around, this symbolic resource was used to extract money from the government rather than private foundations. Nonetheless, it was used as never before to attract students whose presence could be employed as a justification for additional resources from university administrators.

Sociology became the academic program that absorbed many of the most politically committed students of the era. Moreover, these were among the most intellectually committed students and were the best students that sociology had ever attracted. As Figure 4.7 documents, enrollments in sociology increased spectacularly. The number of baccalaureate degrees awarded annually grew from below 15,000 in 1965, a figure itself more than double that of 10 years before, to more than 35,000 by 1970. At the graduate level, the production of Ph.D.'s also increased as a proportion of the expanded undergraduate population continued on to graduate school (see Figure 4.5).

One effect of this growth was for the professional structure of sociology to expand rapidly, as is evidenced by the increase in American Sociological Association membership figures reported

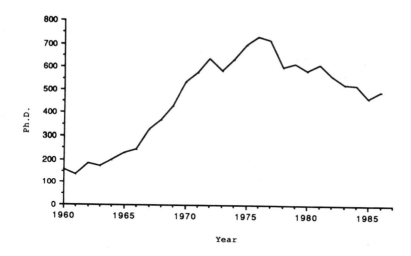

Figure 4.5. Sociology Ph.D.'s 1960 to Present

in Figure 4.8. Sociology had material resources, especially money and student enrollments; it had some symbolic resources, since the problems of the day—race and ethnic tensions, poverty, war, and governmental use/abuse of power—were relevant to sociology. It should not be surprising, therefore, that American sociology sought to mobilize its organizational resources during this period by reorganizing the old American Sociological Society (ASS) into the ASA. Yet, as we come to appreciate, this reorganization did not involve a parallel effort at political and administrative consolidation, centralization, and control. Indeed, it involved just the opposite: the creation of an umbrella organization that would house—indeed, encourage and tolerate—enormous intellectual diversity.

The result was an almost complete inability to consolidate symbolic resources around either a sense of a common professional community—as the founders of American sociology tried to do—or a common corpus and storehouse of knowledge. And when the period of decline in funding, student enrollments, ASA

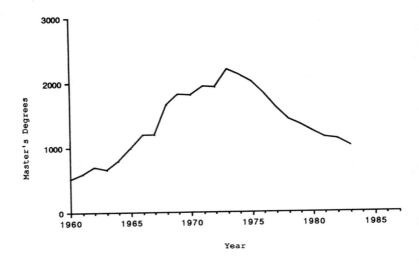

Figure 4.6. Sociology Master's Degrees 1960 to Present

membership, and eventually Ph.D. production began in the mid-1970s, sociology did not have the organizational resources, such as centralized administration and control, nor the symbolic resources, such as common professional identification, consensus over a knowledge base, and prestige within the academic or lay community, to cope with the decline. Nor did the period of decline stimulate efforts to reorganize the discipline or mobilize the profession toward a more coherent conception of itself as a discipline. Again, just the opposite occurred: growth stimulated differentiation and diversity, but decline did not encourage consolidation of resources; in fact, decline encouraged even further differentiation and diversity, partly as a result of inertia but also, significantly, as a result of trying to sustain (or decrease the decline in) membership in ASA by giving anybody and everybody a niche in sociology.

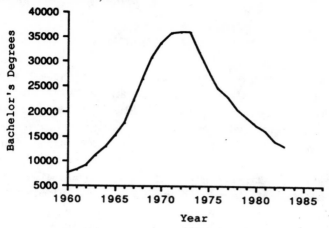

Figure 4.7. Sociology Bachelor's Degrees 1960 to Present

Such was the pattern of growth in American sociology in the post-Sputnik era, at least in broad strokes. Let us now backtrack and fill in this profile in more detail.

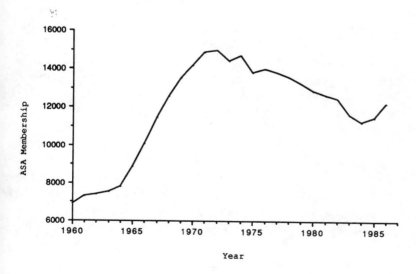

Figure 4.8. ASA Membership 1960 to Present

THE CHANGING BASE
OF MATERIAL RESOURCES

The expansion of federal funding for social research in the 1960s meant that the problems of relating to foundations and private donors were immensely simplified, at least in one respect: academic sociologists now dealt primarily with persons who were bureaucrats with limited ranges of autonomy and interest as well as little desire to exercise the kind of snaffle-and-bit control over social scientists' work that the Carnegie Corporation and private contractors had sometimes exercised. To gain federal funds, organizations like Lazarsfeld's Bureau of Applied Social Research (BASR) did not need to exert the same effort in maintaining cordial relationships and establishing contacts through self-promoting activities.

For a time, the community of foundation officers and entrenched academics simply took over the machinery of distributing federal funding by serving on panels and advising. In time, and with the expansion of support for social research in a variety of agencies of the government, this power was more broadly distributed. In many agencies, proposals for grants were evaluated through "peer review" procedures, in which the standards of the profession were employed, at least within the guidelines of the grant program. In many agencies, decisions were made by former academics who had taken long-term or short-term administrative positions in government. Thus, although the ways in which funds were distributed varied a great deal, decisions tended to increase the role of the professional community or some segment of it. Yet, aside from the "pure" agencies, such as the National Science Foundation (NSF) and to some extent the National Endowment for the Humanities, the procedures did not directly reproduce disciplinary standards. Panels for review in the area of health research, for example, were organized topically, and each area developed its own coterie of "experts," sometimes favorable to some particular style of sociological research, but interdisciplinary in composition. Thus the funding for "sociological" projects by these agencies often required expert evaluation by nonsociologists, a hurdle that had distinctive selective biases that were sometimes at variance with those of the discipline of sociology itself. The panels of private foundations, which were generally smaller than government agencies, were also likely to be less disciplinary in character; here, as well, the credibility of the sociologist's proposal and past work to nonsociological academics were important to success, with the consequence that the selective biases were often at variance with the model of quantitative sociology exemplified in the "leading journals." The constituting documents and statement of purpose of the National Endowment of the Humanities, which is not a lavishly financed organization but nonetheless a source of prestige in the academic community beyond sociology, recognized the methodological conflicts: review panels for sociological work on the large fellowship programs of this agency had, and still have, sociologists, but these tend to be sociologists with reputations for the use of the "methods of the humanities."

In some agencies, especially the military (which supported a considerable amount of research with very little practical utility during this period), the decisions were made even less bureaucratically, often on the basis of personal relationships that a granting officer in some agency, such as the Office of Naval Research, had developed with academics working in some general area in which the agency had an interest. Decisions were typical placed in the hands of persons low in the bureaucratic hierarchy; these persons were likely to accept, in a general way, the standards of the profession, especially as they were indirectly embodied in prestige hierarchies of universities. The faith of the military in the social sciences, or at least its willingness to spend, was extraordinary. In fact, the four branches of the service actually competed to finance "behavioral science" projects, a competition that led to the politically disastrous Project Camelot.

Although much of the federal government's support for graduate education in the 1960s involved fellowships for the living expenses and tuition of graduate students, a large portion of the support took the form of "training grants." These grants, which provided "seed money" for programs of graduate education in areas of presumed long-term practical value, also subsidized tuition and living expenses. For example, a significant amount of money was given to sociologists to develop programs in medical schools to train medical students in the relevant findings and ideas of the behavioral sciences and to equip sociologists to meet the demand for this kind of training. This process greatly expanded the present field of "medical sociology"—by far the largest specialty in sociology.

Direct subsidies to students for graduate education were the first victims of the rather limited financial "austerity" for the sciences introduced in the early 1970s, by the Nixon administration. Other reductions directly targeted at the social sciences, and particularly sociology, were to follow. The character of this change was peculiarly reminiscent of the collapse of Rockefeller support during the 1930s (see Chapter 2). Financing for "basic" research in the social sciences, evaluated by peers, had always been justified by promises of useful results, which were made in the 1960s to activist politicians eager to find means of state intervention into specific social problems. In an atmosphere of greater skepticism about the results of the expensive government programs of intervention, the promises were reassessed. The work done by sociologists in the 1960s was seen to be of little practical value, just as earlier work had been seen by the dissatisfied Rockefeller almoners in the late 1920s and early 1930s. The Nixon administration proposed to transfer some monies used by the NSF to finance sociology to a new program called RANN (Research Applied to National Needs). This proposal was the beginning of a tightening of administrative control over social science funding that ultimately extended even to such agencies as the National Endowment for the Humanities, which, in the Reagan years, sharply reduced funding for disciplines such as sociology that are outside the core disciplines of the humanities. In other agencies, the rates of expenditure for social research were reduced as well. Thus the garden that had blossomed so luxuriantly during the boom times of the 1960s was plowed under.

One immediate consequence of the shift away from "basic" research under the control of academic evaluators was a search for alternative sources of funds within the federal bureaucracy itself. Ironically, one source of funds was the same dissatisfaction with state intervention that was part of the reason for reductions in the funding of the social sciences in the first place. This source was embodied in the desire to demonstrate the effectiveness (or ineffectiveness) of federal social programs. The affinity of bureaucrats for quantitative evidence based on bureaucratic records led to a period in which sociologists competed with accounting firms and other researchers for "evaluation research" projects. Figures like Lazarsfeld, who were veterans of the older forms of client-centered social research, and his students, such as James Coleman and Peter Rossi, emerged as spokesmen of a reorientation to "policy research" designed by quantitatively oriented sociologists to provide empirical warrants for premises supplied by "policymakers."

These activities were designed, in part, to secure funds for the large research shops that had been established during the previous period and, in part, to supply employment for sociologists in the face of the collapse of the academic job market in the 1970s. These efforts gained the enthusiastic support of the ASA, as did intense and expensive lobbying efforts in Congress to save social science funding. But these efforts were never relevant to more than the small group of sociologists employed by consulting agencies and the small number of sociologists with suitably equipped shops. In any event, the character of competition for these research contracts did not favor these shops; rather, they favored Washington-based research units with strong bureaucratic connections and with the ability to shift interests as the political priorities of funding agencies changed. In the long run, academic sociologists simply could not compete against these agencies; moreover, the kinds of analysis commanded by the contracts rarely required quantitative skills distinctive to sociology. Where quantitative estimates of the consequences of decision alternatives were demanded, the methods of econometrics were more appropriate. Where large-scale handling of government data was required, accounting firms were better equipped. Where generic behavioral science research skills were needed, psychologists, statisticians, and persons trained in various applied areas, such as public health, were equally well equipped and often better able to communicate with larger technical audiences. And in general the rise of a survey research industry made the special contribution of the academic sociologists less and less important. Other users of social science methods, such as marketers and pollsters, developed distinctive bodies of relevant expertise and were not compelled to rely on the skills of the "behavioral scientists."

A large group of grant-program decisions, most of which took place in the early 1970s, had significant consequences for enrollments in sociology. Prior to this time, sociology departments had operated as residual social sciences, often taking responsibility for topics and programs, such as gerontology, that were insufficiently large or insufficiently coherent to become an independent discipline. During the 1970s, for example, a large number of programs in "criminal justice" were created under special grants designed to serve as seed money for what would become autonomous programs supported by student demand. Police departments and other agencies involved in such activities as probation and the supervision of juvenile offenders subsidized many of these programs by making degree holders eligible for salary increases and promotions. These programs typically employed some sociologists and drew students from one of sociology's traditional sources. But the creation of these separate programs caused a loss of students from the course sequence leading through graduate school. Afro-American Studies and Women's Studies programs, which were generally not grant created, followed the topical programs in developing their own intellectual, organizational, and curricular structures outside of sociology. Some of these programs did not survive, and, in many cases, when the initial incentives and seed money disappeared, so did the program. Nevertheless, some of the programs prospered. In some universities, criminal justice programs began to serve the earlier purpose of the sociology baccalaureate as an general education degree that gave some access to a wide range of public sector positions. Yet the criminal justice degree could be treated as a preferred degree by agencies concerned with crime, thereby placing its holders in an advantageous position in relation to general sociology students.

A similar kind of competition developed with social work departments, which also faced enrollment losses at the end of the 1970s' boom. In the past, social work training had been given only on the graduate level, with the sociology baccalaureate serving as a common feeder degree. In the 1970s, spurred in part by an obscure federal regulation that specified employment preferences for persons with specialized degrees for entry-level positions in federally supported programs (which included virtually all welfare programs in the United States), social work departments began to grant and accredit baccalaureate "professional" degrees, thus drawing students from another of sociology's traditional constituencies (Bromley and Weed, 1979). These shifts of student demand do not account for the dramatic drop in sociology enrollments at the end of the 1970s' boom. Nevertheless, they mean that if student demand was to return to the levels and mix of the 1950s, sociology programs would not be the destination for many students, since these newer programs, none of which existed in the 1950s, would attract a sizable proportion of the students. There can be, in short, no return to the 1950s; sociology enrollments in the future will have to be based on a different mix of students, with a somewhat different set of motivations from those in the past.

THE REDISTRIBUTION OF ORGANIZATIONAL RESOURCES

The growth in sociology's material resource base stimulated a number of shifts in the instruction of organizational resources: (1) a dramatic differentiation, bordering on fragmentation, of the discipline into an increasing number of substantive subfields; (2) a growth in the number of specialty associations, journals, and regional associations; and (3) a differentiation of the

ASA into an escalated number of sections and activities overseen by a greatly expanded staff.

The Differentiation of the American Sociological Society and Association

In its early years, the ASS devoted most of its efforts to holding an annual meeting and to promoting the development of the social sciences in general and, to a lesser extent, the humanities. In the first two decades, the society helped create the Social Science Research Council (SSRC), *The Encyclopedia of the Social Sciences*, and the American Council of Learned Societies. It also endorsed the founding of a national honorary society. And it lobbied to have the federal government remove the job classification of sociologists as "clerical, administrative, and fiscal service."

But these activities were not far-reaching, and the general thrust of the organization was "the encouragement of sociological research and discussion, and the promotion of intercourse between persons engaged in the scientific study of society" (quoted in Rhoades, 1981, p. 11). Yet the early growth of the society created a number of changes: its budget quadrupled; the number of committees increased from 3 to 10; an accumulating deficit forced an increase in dues (Rhoades, 1981, p. 11); and a procedure for establishing sections was established, although this was to change radically in the 1960s. These early signs of growth and differentiation were accompanied by a variety of integrative strains, both organizationally and intellectually.

Organizationally, the problem of how to organize and administer the society's business more effectively and rationally began to surface, although this problem was only later to become paramount. There was also the debate over how big an organization ASS should be and how it should coordinate its activities with respect to regions, the federal government, and international organizations. Additionally, concern over who could be a member, and the appropriate credentials for such membership, was becoming an issue. Moreover, the size, the diversity, and the sections' role in the annual meeting were becoming an administrative problem. And, as we noted earlier, the continuation of the University of Chicago's *American Journal of Sociology* (*AJS*) as the official journal of the society was beginning to be viewed as detrimental to the discipline. In spite of the fact that the journal was losing money and thereby being subsidized by ASS members, the membership nonetheless supported a new journal for the society.

Intellectually, the problems of ASS were perhaps more pronounced. By 1930, the relationship between the applied and purely scientific character of sociological research and knowledge was beginning to be debated and to divide sociologists. Should sociology be a pure science, or should it be more applied and actively seek to orient its research to social problems?

Both these organizational and intellectual problems were approached in a manner typical of voluntary organizations that meet annually and have no real professional/bureaucratic staff: committees were appointed to study the problems and issue reports. As early as 1932, the Scope Research Committee proposed a new constitution for the society. As Rhoades summarizes (1981, p. 30), the key elements of their proposal were to keep membership open, recognize sections, create a board of directors as the governing body, assign the Executive Committee specific policy-making powers, create a full-time executive secretary, and require a two-thirds vote of members for constitutional amendments. A year later, a new committee on the Revision of the Constitution proposed and had accepted by the society a constitution that took a far more conservative route. The major structural changes of the new constitution were to: (1) continue the practice of electing members of the Executive Committee as the governing body of the society; (2) require the president, secretary, and section chairs to meet in order to coordinate plans for the national meeting; and (3) affirm the principle of majority vote for approval of constitutional amendments. As a result of this last provision, a number of amendments were added in the next years, the most important being the establishment of an editorial board for the *American Sociological Review* (*ASR*), which another committee had recommended in 1935. Official ties to the *AJS* were severed, with the result that the society had created the precedent for publishing its own journals.

The other significant structural change was initiated by the Executive Committee to charter local and regional "groups of ten or more persons at least one of whom shall be a member of the American Sociological Society." But, as we will document shortly, this uneasy liaison between the regionals and the national association was soon undone, placing the national organization on a path of expanding its sections.

Perhaps the most troublesome issue of the 1930s, however, was the intellectual debate over applied versus pure science. A group of sociologists, including P. A. Sorokin and R. M. MacIver, quoted the ASS's constitution's emphasis on "the *scientific* study of society" to recommend consolidating the control structure of the society to emphasize science and to reduce outside pressures on sociologists to study social problems. Their specific proposals included the imposition by the society of more rigorous membership standards and the control by the society of all sociological journals. These proposals were, as is typical of voluntary organizations, delegated to various committees for further study. The Special Committee on the Scope of Sociology defended applied sociology, but its recommendations were very much in tune with its critics—centralized control by the society of its programs and serious efforts to exclude nonsociological organizations from sociological research. Its recommendations were placed in a proposed constitution, the key elements of which were summarized above.

What is crucial here is that problems of growth and diversity were creating pressures in the 1930s for consolidation and control by the ASS. There were, however, limits to how much control could be generated by a voluntary organization with no administrative staff and headquarters. Moreover, the "liberal individualism" of professional sociologists, especially those of this early period, placed severe constraints on just how much control they would allow the ASS to assume. Thus, it was only when the ASS, and later the ASA, grew in the post-World War II era that the

society could make this transition to a more differentiated bureaucratic structure. And even then, as we explore in the next
chapter, the control exerted by the ASA is rather minimal, especially when compared to other sciences.

In 1948, the ASS doubled its membership but was still a relatively small organization of less than 2500 members. Yet, a special
ad hoc committee reported that

> the present administrative arrangements for conducting the
> Society's business are inadequate to handle that business
> properly in the interests of the members . . . the committee
> believes that the problem of a more adequate management
> is but one part of a much needed integration to reorganiza-
> tion in the interests of the sociological profession. (quoted
> in Rhoades, 1981)

The committee's recommendation eventually led to yet another committee which, in 1949, reported a need for "greater
continuity and carrying out of the work of the Society; greater
recognition of the needs of specialized groups within the Society;
and an executive staff, either a paid secretary or a paid secretar-
iat" (quoted in Rhoades, 1981). This recommendation led to the
use of a small grant from the Carnegie Corporation to establish a
part-time officer and an executive office, which was initially
located at Columbia and then moved to New York University.
The first executive officer was Matilda White Riley, who served
until 1960. Irene Tauber was the volunteer secretary-treasurer.
There was a small budget for hourly secretarial help, although as
the 1950s came to a close, a full-time secretary was appointed.

In 1960, the ASS was thus a very small organization. John Riley,
Matilda White Riley's husband and secretary-treasurer of ASA
for much of the 1960s, offers several anecdotes to illustrate just
how small the society was. In 1949, when the ASS was making
the move to New York, he drove a station wagon to Washington,
DC, and picked up the entire body of records for the society—a
total of four drawers. In 1950, when the first annual meeting
west of the Mississippi was held in Denver, Colorado, John and

Matilda Riley packed their two kids, camping gear, all the administrative materials necessary to register everyone, and books from publishers for display into their car and set off for the meetings, which were held in a second-rate hotel. Riley recalls that they spent the night setting up registration tables and book displays while writing a skit for presentation the next day. The great fear was that no one would come, but in fact 400 showed up, which, at the time, was a considerable number.

The period between 1950 and 1970 was, in Lawrence Rhoades's words, the "Golden Era" of American sociology (1981, p. 42). We saw the beginnings of this era in the last chapter, but the 1960s accelerated the activities of ASS, soon to be ASA. Membership increased dramatically; revenues increased correspondingly; annual meeting attendance went from 400 to more than 3000; the number of papers read grew from 100 to many hundreds; from a mere handful, more than 650 members now sat on the committees and boards; ASR submissions jumped from 200 to 800 a year; and the society and association began to take on, acquire, and create new journals—a trend only reversed in the last few years.

The growth and expanded activity was reflected in, and caused by, changes in the society. The first change was its name to the American Sociological Association, which, in a sense, connotes a broader base of representation and a less intimate and cohesive form of organization. More fundamentally, the constitution was changed in a number of ways, the net effect of which was to: (1) strengthen the executive office, (2) expand the association's activities—awards, journals, nonjournal publications, fellowships, etc.—and (3) create the current system of year-round sections in various specialized fields. In turn, these changes led to further changes, which culminated in moving the executive office to Washington, DC, remunerating a full-time executive officer, expanding new programs and initiatives (fellowships, small grants, lobbying, formation of new committees and caucuses, etc.), severing the last formal ties to local and regional associations, revising the dues structure, expanding the administrative staff at the executive office, and purchasing a headquarters for the association.

Prior to 1963, when ASA moved to Washington, DC, it was still a very small organization in bureaucratic terms. But with the move, things began to change. Gresham Sykes, who was the first executive officer under the reorganized ASA in 1963, reports that the staff consisted of the executive officer, an administrative assistant, and one secretary. By the time he left in 1963, the "bureaucratic writing was on the wall," for the secretarial staff had increased to eight, and a half-time position was added to organize the annual meeting. Sykes reports that these early changes reflected the views of senior scholars, most notably Talcott Parsons, that sociology should be organized more like psychology—big, inclusive, and powerful. In their view, the ASA should be able to increase the stature and standing of sociology in the lay, scientific, and governmental communities. The result was a rapid decline in the "club-like" and "informal" atmosphere to a more formal, centralized bureaucratic profession. Indeed, as John Riley recalls of the 1950s, "everybody knew everyone," for "the Society was like a family, a gemeinschaft!" Such was no longer to be the case.

Today, ASA is a much larger organization with an executive officer, full-time professional staff, many diverse sections, an expanded number of committees, an increased number of elected positions/officers, a number of journals, and a broad range of service activities, such as grants, fellowships, lobbying efforts, and so on.

The greatest amounts of growth and differentiation in ASA have been in the administrative staff, the number of sections, and the number of journals, although in 1988, there was an effort to shed the administration and financing of several journals that were seen to represent a drain on resources (however, ASA still controls the appointment of the editor of these journals). There appears to be a decline in the number of standing committees, which is perhaps to be expected as the expanded professional staff assumes much of the burden of volunteer labor on the old standing committees.

While much of this organizational differentiation represents a response to the needs of an ever-increasing diversity of sociologists, it also can be viewed as an effort by the ASA to mobilize organizational resources and co-opt as large a segment of professional sociology as it could. That is, by offering something for everyone, the ASA hoped to gain a measure of hegemony, and to remain more than *primus inter pares* among the other regional and specialized professional associations to which sociologists belong. In addition to these co-optive efforts, ASA is like all organizations in that the emerging ASA bureaucracy creates its own needs to expand. It does so by extending the scope of its activities and then using these efforts at extension to justify increased dues to support a larger staff.

To some extent, the expansion of ASA activities may have been somewhat counterproductive, escalated dues may have led some sociologists to drop their membership, although much of the membership loss from 1975 to 1985 reflects a drop in highly subsidized student memberships as job-market conditions reduced the number of sociology graduate students. More fundamental in the long run, however, is the fact that ASA is in an increasingly competitive situation with specialty associations, which many practitioners find more professionally useful and interesting than either the large ASA annual conventions or the ASA journals (although ASA's expansion of its sections and journal offerings represents one effort to meet this competition).

At present ASA may have reached the limits of its growth and differentiation cycle: it cannot grow without further increases in dues or cutbacks in expensive projects, such as journals, fellowships, and grants. But if it reduces its involvement in such projects, it may lose more members. And, if it raises dues to sustain these activities, it will also begin to lose those members who are at their financial limit with the current dues structure.

Moreover, as ASA conventions become large brokerage affairs—a far cry from the old "club-like" atmosphere that John Riley describes—many sociologists choose not to attend the national meeting, preferring instead to go to smaller specialty meetings where they know more people and have more interests in common. So even if the dues structure was not an issue, sociologists' prime loyalties are often to organizations other than ASA. Thus, given its competitive situation, there are limits to the capacity of ASA to mobilize organizational resources.

The Regional Associations

At the early point in the growth of sociology right after World War II, there were four major regional associations: the Pacific Sociological Association (founded around 1929-1931), the Mid-western Sociological Society (1936-1937), the Southern Sociological Society (1935-1938), and the Eastern Sociological Society (1930). Because of name changes in these organizations (see Hetrick, Pease, and Mathers, 1978), there is some confusion as to the exact dates when these organizations emerged, but in general terms the regional associations were created in the 1930s. In addition to these major associations, several other prominent regional associations were also created in this period, including the District of Columbia Sociological Society (1930-1944), the Southwestern Sociological Association (1937-1938), and the North Central Sociological Association (which was established in 1938, although its predecessor—the Ohio Sociological Society— was founded in 1925 and later expanded to the Ohio Valley Sociological Society which, in 1972, was renamed the North Central Sociological Association). Thus, even when national ASA membership was low, ranging from 1000 to 1500, viable regional associations were in place. Indeed, while figures are unavailable, regional membership was probably much higher before World War II than membership in the national association. In particular, the Depression saw a 33% decline in ASA membership, while regional associations remained more active (primarily in light of the costs of travel during economically difficult times).

The regional associations had a vacillating relationship with the old ASS, and later, with the ASA. In 1932, the ASS amended its constitution to allow "the establishment of regional chapters." The result was the affiliation of "sociology clubs" and various regional associations with ASS. Until 1934, when the first regional joined the ASS, there was no formal relationship between regionals and the national. From 1934 to 1946, regional associations were chapter members of ASS, but it was between 1942 and 1962 that the regionals exerted the most influence on ASS/ASA. During this period, the seven major regional associations were entitled to elect one member to the council of the national organization. Since the council is its major policy-making branch, the regionals could exert considerable influence on the national association. But in 1963, as the national association was beginning to reorganize, the regionals were restricted to nominating candidates, with only ASA members actually voting on them. This practice lasted until 1967, at which time even this form of regional input was terminated. Since 1968, ASA has had an inactive committee on "regional affairs," and recently there have been proposals to abolish this committee.

In should respects, however, the regional societies serve as organizational resources and provide offices, honors, and organizational roles for many sociologists excluded from the political leadership core of the ASA. The regional meetings are not only smaller, but *gemeinschaftliche* in tone, as the ASA is not. The proliferation of sections of the ASA also has provided some organizational structures with some of the ambience of a smaller organization, and sometimes the sections serve as an organizational base for a heterodox movement or specialty distant from the "mainstream" that nevertheless wishes to preserve its claim on legitimacy as a part of sociology. Several of the recently established sections, such as the Sociology of Emotions, Sociology of Knowledge and Technology, and Sociology of Culture, were largely motivated by this aim and by the difficulty of arranging for paper sessions on the main program. In some cases, the regional societies have served as loci for heterodox movements. For example, symbolic interactionism is well entrenched in the Midwest Sociological Society; various nonstandard forms of ethnomethodology were once entrenched in the Pacific Sociological Society. The symbolic interactionists have their own society and journal, and the ethnomethodologists and conversational analysts meet annually in a small but intense workshop/conference. As a result, their attachment to regionals has declined.

Yet while the major regional associations find themselves in increased competition with various subregionals, specialty associations, and sections of ASA, they still provide an organization resource—offices, honors, reading of papers, network ties, and the like—for many sociologists who are not part of the ASA system. Of course, the ASA has sought, under the symbolism of "democratization," to increase the number and diversity of participants in sections, sessions, and committees, but the vast majority of sociologists are still uninvolved. The regional associations provide an alternative, and the competition between the well-organized but remote ASA, on the one side, and the poorly organized but more immediate regionals, on the other, should be interesting. Yet both may suffer from the growth of specialty associations.

The Proliferation of Subfields and Specialty Associations

The organizational differentiation of the ASA reflects, more than it has caused, the proliferation of subfields and specialties. Based on the ASA official index, there are more than 50 fields of specialization in which graduate instruction is offered. There is, in a very real sense, a specialty for everyone in American sociology, particularly when it is recognized that there are multiple subspecialties for each of these 50 or so "main" areas of specialization.

It is natural that professionals working within a given subfield or topic area should want to communicate with each other. As sociology has grown and differentiated into an expanding number of specialized fields, therefore, it is inevitable that practitioners in these specialties would organize meetings and, in some cases, publish journals. Some of these specialty associations are interdisciplinary, but many are organized primarily for sociologists.

To some extent, the growth in the number of ASA sections and journals represents a response to this need for contact among specialists, but there are limits to how far ASA can go in proliferating sections, if only because of its limited membership. The regionals, which simply do not have the financial or organizational resources to create and sustain a large number of active sections, cannot meet these needs of specialists, save for creating specialized sessions at their annual meetings.

A perusal of announcements of annual meetings in ASA's *Footnotes* and other sources reveals that there are presently approximately 40 specialty associations in America (excluding "international" associations). We are sure, however, that there are more associations, but even this number indicates that American sociology is differentiated into many specialty associations, many of which are larger than some of the major regional associations. It is not unreasonable to conclude, therefore, that there is a specialty association for almost every kind of sociologist. Moreover, a good many of these associations do what the ASA does—offer annual meetings, newsletters, and journals to fellow specialists—and so it is not surprising that many sociologists—indeed, perhaps the majority—find participation in these specialty associations more interesting, enjoyable, and professionally profitable than involvement in either the national or regional associations.

Such specialty associations, however, encourage the partitioning of sociology into a large number of discrete and unintegrated subfields where scholars can literally "go their own way" and "pursue what pleases them" without great concern about where their work and interests fit into the broader field of sociology. Eventually, the upper limit as to how many of these associations can exist will be reached, given the absolute number of professional sociologists available, but we suspect that even the current number does not come close to this limit. We can, therefore, look forward to further differentiation of sociology around specialty associations.

The Proliferation of Journals

In 1933, there were 9 scholarly journals of sociology for academic sociologists. As one would expect, the growth in number and specialization of sociologists has caused the number and variety of journals to expand dramatically in the 50-plus years since that time. In fact, there is no complete list of sociology journals in America, although Wespsiec's (1983) is reasonably comprehensive. But by even the most conservative estimate there are more than 200 journals (excluding all foreign journals) that are primarily sociological in their content. If one adds journals published outside the United States, then the number of journals for sociologists is probably greater than 300.

The number and diversity of journals provide a research outlet for virtually every kind of intellectual activity. While the most prestigious journals are controlled by ASA, the regional associations, and a few key specialty associations, this control applies to only a handful of the many research outlets in America and is, therefore, very limited. Moreover, although some journals fail, the trend is for a net increase in research outlets, even as the number of professionally active sociologists stabilizes or declines.

The existence of so many journals, most of which are specialized, further partitions American sociology in many different directions: subject matter, methodology, ideology, and theoretical persuasion. And it greatly diffuses reputational resources. The major national journals—ASR and AJS—plus the principal regional journals are still general, although they have biases toward certain topics, methodologies, and theoretical approaches. Even with these biases, which are toward quantitative methodology and metatheory, and even with the prestige that they bestow on those who publish in them, they are not an effective mechanism for integrating sociological research. Scholars can still achieve prominence and reap the professional rewards that come with publishing when placing their works in less prestigious specialty journals, especially since their most relevant cohort or reference group is more likely to read the specialty journal than the general brokerage journals of either ASA or the regional associations.

The Expanding Teaching Curriculum

Table 4.1 reproduces the chapter titles of the most representative introductory sociology texts, starting with the very first one in 1894, moving through the most prominent and representative of the pre- and post-World War II era, and ending with the current "best-seller." Of course, chapter titles are only a very rough indicator of what is inside a book, although after considerable effort at finding an alternative basis of comparison, we concluded that, in the end, this was the best procedure for getting a sense of how sociology is taught.

Probably the first "modern" text is Kingsley Davis's *Human Society* (1948). A comparison of its chapter titles with the most recent texts reveals relatively few differences. There is an opening chapter on what sociology is, then a concern with micro processes and the individual/personality in society, a brief social psychological analysis of deviance, a review of structural units (groups, communities, classes, and the like), a summary of major institutions, and a closing hodge-podge on social change and demography. If one compares chapter titles between the early and later eras, one big difference is the emphasis on social processes in earlier texts; they were much more concerned with social forces and process than with structure. Moreover, they are far more analytical than modern texts, trying to describe the basic and fundamental properties of society. Part of the reason for this difference is that the early texts were still very much under the

Table 4.1 Chapter Titles of Prominent Introductory Sociology Texts, 1894–1986

Albion W. Small and George E. Vincent *An Introduction to the Study of Society* (1894)	Frank Lester Ward *Outlines of Sociology* (1897)	Edward Alsworth Ross *Foundations of Sociology* (1905)
The Beginning of Sociology	The Place of Sociology Among the Sciences	The Scope and Task of Sociology
The Development of Sociology	Relation of Sociology to Cosmology	The Sociological Frontier of Economics
The Relation of Sociology to the Special Social Sciences	Relation of Sociology to Biology	Social Laws
The Relation of Sociology to Social Reforms	Relation of Sociology to Anthropology	The Unit of Investigation in Sociology
The Organic Conception of Society	Relation of Sociology to Psychology	Mob Mind
The Family on the Farm	The Data of Sociology	The Properties of Group-Units
The Rural Group	The Social Forces	The Social Forces
The Village	The Mechanics of Sociology	The Factors of Social Change
Town and City	The Purpose of Sociology	Recent Trends in Sociology
The Social Elements: Land and Population	Individual Telesis	The Causes of Race Superiority
The Primary Social Group	Collective Telesis	The Value Rank of the American People
Social Aggregates and Organs		
The Psycho-physical Communicating Apparatus		
The Life of Society in General: The Functions of the Family		
The Functions of the Society as Performed by Organs		
Pathology in General		
The Pathology of Social Organs		
The Phenomena of Social Psychology in General		
Social Consciousness—the Phenomena of Authority		
Certain Laws of Social Psychology—Social Intelligence and Feeling		
Social Volition and Execution—Morality and Law		
Recapitulation		

(Continued)

Table 4.1 Chapter Titles of Prominent Introductory Sociology Texts, 1894–1986 (Continued)

Robert E. Park and Ernest W. Burgess *Introduction to the Science of Sociology* (1921)	*Kingsley Davis* *Human Society* (1948)	*Leonard Broom and Philip Selznick* *Sociology: A Text with Adapted Readings* (1973)
Sociology and the Social Sciences	The Study of Human Society	Introduction
Human Nature	Human versus Animal Society	Social Organization
Investigations and Problems	Social Norms	Culture
Society and the Group	Status and Role	Socialization
Isolation	The Elements of Social Action	Primary Groups
Social Contacts	Forms of Interaction	Social Stratification
Social Interaction	Jealousy and Sexual Property	Associations
Social Forces	Socialization	Collective Behavior
Competition	Personality Integration	Population
Conflict	Personality Disorganization	The Family
Accommodation	Primary and Secondary Groups	Education
Assimilation	Rural and Urban Communities	Religion
Social Control	The Crowd and the Public	Law
Collective Behavior	Caste, Class, and Stratification	Race and Ethnicity
Progress	Marriage and the Family	Urbanization
	Science, Technology, and Society	Technology and Civilization
	Economic Institutions	Politics and Society
	Political Institutions	
	Religious Institutions	
	The Demographic Equation	
	World Population in Transition	
	The Meaning of Social Change	

(Continued)

Table 4.1 Chapter Titles of Prominent Introductory Sociology Texts, 1894–1986 (Continued)

Ian Robertson
Sociology (3rd edition, 1987)

Sociology: A New Look at a Familiar World
Doing Sociology: The Methods of Research
Culture
Society
Socialization
Social Interaction in Everyday Life
Social Groups
Deviance
Sexuality and Society
Social Stratification
Inequalities of Race and Ethnicity
Inequalities of Gender and Age
The Family
Education
Religion
Medicine
The Economic Order
The Political Order
Social Change
Collective Behavior and Social Movements
Population and Urbanization
Technology and Environment
War and Peace

sway of Comte's positivism and Spencerianism; another part of
the explanation is that early sociologists were trying to establish
both the boundaries and basic units of sociological analysis; yet
another part is that they were more theoretically inclined than
the later generation of text writers; and a final reason for this
difference is that modern texts are driven by more highly competitive student market pressures than the earlier ones were.

But the most noticeable feature of the modern text, compared
to its earlier counterpart, is the "topic" emphasis of current
introductory texts, which might be expected in light of the large
number of subfields. This topic emphasis is not well reflected in
the chapter titles, but within chapters what emerges is a review
of basic findings for substantive subspecialties within sociology—family sociology, social psychology, demography, deviance, crime and delinquency, socialization and personality, small
groups, complex organizations, urban sociology, ethnic relations,
and the "sociology of" religion, education, medicine, science,
law, etc. The grouping of these topics under a common set of
chapters reflects market pressures (the best-selling texts "do it
this way" and so others follow the lead) more than conceptual or
theoretical integration. Indeed, one of the recent "innovations"
of the modern text is the discussion of three or four "theoretical
paradigms" (functional, conflict, interactionist, for example) in
relation to each topic. This effort is, in many ways, a confession
that there is no conceptual or theoretical integration of topics.
Each topic is, in effect, a differentiated subfield, most of whose
practitioners probably find it amusing to have their work analyzed into these alien theoretical (metatheoretical) "paradigms."
This lack of complete conceptual integration was evident from
sociology's beginning, but it accelerated in the 1920s as Herbert
Spencer's star faded and as a more empirical research orientation replaced old macro and global theories (see Chapter 2 for
details).

These changes in introductory texts mirror changes in the
teaching curriculum. Today, sociology is differentiated into far

more topical subfields than it was earlier, and this fact is reflected in the topics within chapters of texts as well as in the course offerings of departments. As was emphasized earlier, a few departments in the early era taught many sociology courses, but today even a small department teaches substantially more courses, as well as a greater variety of courses, than previously. In effect, sociologists can now teach almost anything they want; indeed, virtually any topic is legitimate, especially since "topics in" (almost anything) courses are now part of most college catalogues. Moreover, to question the relevance or importance of course offerings often invites cries of intrusion into scholars' academic freedom. Naturally, universities and departments vary enormously in how much eclecticism they can allow (given the number and areas of expertise in their faculty) and in how much diversity and scope they will tolerate (given the biases of administrative powers). But, having acknowledged this variation, the general trend is for maintaining diversity, with periodic efforts at curriculum consolidation and reform.

Thus, college and university teachers in America have many options in their course offerings. While a market situation or chronic shortage of certain needed personnel in a department often forces teachers to take on courses that they would rather avoid, there is usually a trade-off, and in exchange for offering needed courses, teachers are then given some "of their own." Moreover, the tight job market of the last decade has encouraged diversity, more than squelched it, since migrating pools of temporary lecturers constantly shift the distribution of expertise in a department and hence its list of course offerings.

This diversity in the sociology curriculum is particularly significant because the vast majority of sociologists view themselves as teachers. While the elite core and semi-core of universities with Ph.D. graduate programs are research oriented, there are more than 10 times as many teaching-oriented colleges and universities. These teachers thus have as many, and perhaps more, professional options than do university-based researchers, who are often constrained by the dictates of funding agencies, by the desires of their departments for "certain kinds of research," and by the wish to publish in the "right" journals. Thus, teachers can be more diverse than researchers, because they have more options in "doing their own thing" than research-oriented scholars at the elite core and semi-core. For those who define teaching as their professional calling, then, there are no powerful curricular forces pulling them together and into doing similar work, as was at one time the case in early American sociology programs. Indeed, teachers are often able to teach highly specialized courses, thereby propelling them intellectually away from each other.

Thus, as the curriculum of colleges and universities have diversified, a potentially important organizational resource is not fully utilized as an integrating force. And even general texts, which could provide some symbolic unity, are in fact simply unintegrated summaries of major topic areas and subspecialties within sociology (they look alike not out of conceptual integration but because, as a result of market pressures, they copy each other). Only where the teaching curriculum is narrow and tightly coordinated—and this is very rare at the baccalaureate level—does teaching serve to integrate a departmental faculty. But even when such integration does occur, it is at the department level rather than the *inter*department level, indicating the extent to which organizational resources are dispersed. As a result, it has few consequences for the mobilization of symbolic resources to intellectually integrate the profession nationally. Indeed, most departments have loose curricula, and even those with an integrated curriculum have achieved it in widely different ways.

The diversity of sociology curricula can also be viewed in a more positive light. It signals that the field has indeed established itself within academia, while at the same time fostering a freedom of inquiry and a vitality of thought. But whatever the merits of these arguments, it does not signal either intellectual coherence or structural integration. As we will argue later, this lack of integration has important consequences for the organization and substance of American sociology.

REDISTRIBUTION OF SYMBOLIC RESOURCES

*Efforts at Symbolic Unification
Through Functionalism and the Chaotic Aftermath*

Why was functionalism so successful at the beginning of the modern era? In addition to the intrinsic appeal of Parsons's conceptual scheme, the ideas of functionalism served largely as a framework that legitimated commonplace patterns of explanation. "Theoretical" analyses of a given phenomenon took a simple form: they showed that the phenomenon had, contrary to first appearances, some connection to the larger "goals" or "ends" of the "system" of which it could be described as a part. It was easy to invent such explanations, and it was equally easy to employ the dominant model of research practice to statistically prove "effects." Functional explanations, as supported by correlational techniques documenting "effects," gave sociologists something beyond common sense to say about a great many areas of social life.

The methods and the theories were thus useful devices for staking out disciplinary claims to a phenomenon, but they did not direct cumulative development, because both the methods and explanations could proliferate without consolidation. Indeed, a number of hypotheses about how a given phenomenon might contribute to social functioning could be generated for virtually any of the patterns or institutions sociologists studied, but these were partial explanations which assumed that some sort of broader account of "functioning" could be constructed. Yet, in fact, such functional explanations were often little more than redescriptions of an institution couched in the language of system ends and requisites, and, as it became painfully evident, many different "systems," "ends," and images of "systemic relationships" could be used to complete functional explanations. Moreover, the vogue of operations research, cybernetics and information theory, and the metaphor of self-regulating machines lent a kind of "scientific" legitimacy to these explanations, but at the same time added to the diversity as people began to identify themselves as different kinds of functionalists. And there were few discursive means by which these alternative images could be decisively refuted or consolidated. At most, other explanations could be shown to fit with and connect wider sets of facts. But for the most part, explanations changed by incorporation, not elimination.

By the time of Kingsley Davis's presidential address to the ASA in 1959, it was possible to *identify* functional explanation with sociological explanation—to say that it was a myth that functionalism represented a distinctive form of sociological analysis. Yet at the very time that these confident proclamations were being issued, the dominance of "structural functionalism" and its variants was increasingly challenged within American sociology. Its strongest rivals were approaches that shared some of its key traits. For example, symbolic interactionism, which had by the late 1940s been turned by Blumer into a distinctive "viewpoint," was like functionalism in that it was a vocabulary that could be used to give quick redescriptions of familiar material in a manner beyond common sense. And like functionalism, symbolic interactionism was easy to teach and attractive to students. In addition to symbolic interactionism there was a revival of Marxian analysis, though in the early 1960s it often differed from functional analyses only with respect to the specification of the "ends" served by particular social patterns. But the "conflict" critique of Parsonian theory gained prominence, led by Europeans (Lockwood, 1956; Dahrendorf, 1958) and a few American Marxists (e.g., Mills, 1959). The contents of these critiques varied, but in the 1960s the issues became routinized: according to the critics, functionalism was an ideology supporting the status quo and did not devote sufficient conceptual attention to inequality, power, coercion, conflict, and change. The result was to identify the criticism of functionalism with the New Left, an identity that temporarily aided the critics by attracting students. But the long-term effect was to establish a mode of metatheoretical criticism that held up "accounting for change, power, and conflict" as the explanatory ideal.

As the 1960s progressed and as this "conflict" theoretic critique was joined by other substantive and logical criticisms (see J. H. Turner, 1986; Turner and Maryanski, 1979 for a review), Parsonian functionalism began to fall from favor. As functionalism declined, the older perspectives, which were at the vanguard of the critique of functionalism, began to split off in varying directions. In addition, a wide variety of new theoretical perspectives emerged. The end result was that, in the wake of functionalism's brief moment of domination, a period of eclecticism, diversity, debate, and acrimony came to typify American theory.

Theoretical sociology has moved in many directions over the last three decades. One direction revolves around the continued proliferation of specialty theories, or what J. H. Turner (1985) has called "theories of (pick your favorite substantive topics)." These are theories about some structure, process, or phenomenon— crime, delinquency, sex roles, poverty, family, feminism, urban ecology, attitude change, group dynamics, demographic transitions, personality, economic growth, world system dynamics, societal revolutions, the rise and fall of empires, ethnic relations, class relations, political elites, organizational growth, emotions, and so on for virtually all substantive subfields in sociology. This proliferation of specialty theories is, of course, an extension of the pre-World War II legacy that, after the fall of Spencer and organicism, moved not only to an action approach, but also to narrow theories about specific topics.

Another direction has been the development of more general integrative theories that cut across substantive topics. These theories make claims for being inclusive, but in fact these claims are often excessive as theorists assert that their approach explains all of reality and is *the* only appropriate theoretical strategy. The existence of multiple orientations suggests that it will be difficult to achieve theoretical integration. Moreover, proponents of various orientations often view one another with suspicion, if not acrimony.

Yet another direction is metatheory, which, in a sense, represents an effort to cope with the current theoretical diversity (Ritzer, 1975, 1989). Here, scholars analyze existing theories, seeking to sort out their presuppositions, epistemologies, ontologies, and metaphysics. This metatheorizing can also involve attempts to create a general set of guidelines for all theory. In a sense, metatheory recognizes the fractured and diverse nature of current theories, and it tries to do something about the situation. But the metatheorists' advice is often rather vague and general, often oratorical in character: study acts and interactions, structure and culture. As a result, metatheorists talk primarily to each other, and so metatheorizing has not succeeded as an integrating effort.

A final direction has been an effort to expand existing theoretical orientations, or to create new ones that are more eclectic and pull together elements of other theoretical orientations into a synthesis. For example, the British social theorist Anthony Giddens (1984) has a much more receptive audience in America than in Europe because his "structuration theory" appears to pull together what are often considered very incomparable approaches—structuralism, phenomenology and ethnomethodology, dramaturgy, Marxism, and psychoanalytic theory. But even these eclectic theories create camps, as in the case for Gidden's approach, which antagonizes all positivists as well as the prominent theorists from whom he borrows. Similar fates have awaited others who have sought to be synthetic; they manage to antagonize some ad hoc coalition of very strange bedfellows who are offended by some inappropriate use of "their" ideas.

Thus, while these recent synthetic theories and the present popularity of metatheorizing signal a thirst for some kind of conceptual unity, these efforts have not been successful. And even when they win converts, those converts are usually members of the theoretical community—a rather small group of 500 to 600. The result is that most American sociologists, especially research-oriented sociologists, do not pay much attention to what are seen as vague, excessively abstract, and arcane pronouncements from general theorists. If they are inclined toward theory at all, empirical researchers feel much happier with narrow "theories of" than with the more integrative efforts of general theorists.

The post-Parsonian period thus reveals a growing split between "theorists' theory" and "researchers' theory." Moreover, there appears to be an expanding variety of partitions within theory itself. The new partitions not only reflect substantive commitments but also strategic and philosophical commitments. Some believe that laws of human organization can be developed; others view the very nature of human organization as changeable by human agency, and hence not subject to invariant laws. Some argue for metatheory, others for deductive systems of propositions, still others for discursive analyses, and yet another group for formal models. Some argue that theory must begin with micro processes, others just the reverse. And so it goes. It is perhaps not surprising, therefore, that researchers simply throw up their hands at theorists and get on with the process of collecting data.

But this split between theory and research assures that sociology will remain not only differentiated but intellectually fragmented. Researchers and theorists rarely talk to each other, and within theoretical sociology, there are unending debates and arguments. This situation is sustained, indeed reinforced, by the dispersal of organizational, material, and reputational resources. For example, the structure of ASA tries to accommodate everyone, although there is a bias for quantitative over qualitative research in the organizational hierarchy. Seeking compromise, synthesis, or consensus is simply not necessary, however, since there are sections within the ASA for very different approaches, and if the ASA cannot accommodate an approach, there is a friendly specialty journal or association that will. Thus, intellectual diversity and the organization of American sociology are mutually reinforcing.

In light of this dispersal of resources, especially as reflected in the diversity of theoretical approaches, it will be difficult for American sociology to become theoretically unified like the natural sciences—a fact that underscores the title of this book. Indeed, as a sign of this diversity, many theorists would even question this criterion—mature science—as relevant to sociology. Thus, to the extent that intellectual unification has occurred in

American sociology, it is not through theory but through the rise of quantitative methods in this century, although consensus over appropriateness and use of such methods is far from complete.

Efforts at Symbolic Unification
Through Multivariate Methods

The huge and totally unprecedented graduate enrollments of the late 1960s enabled sociologists to be more selective about students, and to some extent there was more selectivity than ever before, but this selectivity was peculiarly distributed. The criteria on which selection at the graduate level was made tended to be not so much for general cultural literacy but for statistical ability. Moreover, the same kind of selectivity occurred at the level of tenure: many American universities became ambitious to rise in relative status during this period and pursued this by instituting a system of "publish or perish." This was the key to the "academic revolution," which placed faculty members even in minor universities more than ever under the influence of national disciplinary standards and expectations. This system favored, and heavily favored, the sociologist who was capable of producing a large number of articles in respectable journals of sociology.

Competition for space in these journals, itself largely a new phenomenon, heavily favored statistical work. The more statistical and routinized the papers became, the more likely they were to get in a major journal, and even the minor journals began to emulate the more prestigious ones, with the result that sociological papers in both major and minor journals look much the same. From the point of view of the author, the acceptance of these papers was more easily defended against criticism. In each of the social sciences a pecking order of journals was established, and journals were valued in terms of the pecking order both by authors ambitious for a respectable record of publication and editors concerned with their standing in the pecking order.

One thus need not adduce any complex intellectual reasons for the rapid increase in the proportion of work of a statistical character in the "best" journals and for the effects of this newly competitive environment on graduate programs. Defendants that sought to maintain their standing in the profession employed young sociologists who could produce these articles, and they argued for changes in graduate requirements that would assure that the graduates of the leading universities would be able to produce articles of this kind. These changes, in turn, demanded the employment of more young faculty capable of training graduate students in these methods, with competition for these faculty resulting in even more extreme increases in requirements. And the increased competition for space in the best journals escalated the statistical refinements of submitted work. As a result, the old SSRC goal of the 1930s for increasing the statistical content of graduate education in the social sciences was finally realized.

The complexities were evident, however, in some of the consequences of the conjunction of the hierarchical differentiation of the field and increased reliance on statistical methods. There were long-standing ideological or "cultural" reasons for and against the use of statistics and especially over the identification of statistics with the hope of making sociology a "science." These had already been manifested in departmental political struggles. The 1950s had seen a bitter battle for the control of the department at Chicago, won by the statistically oriented sociologists. The 1960s saw a series of battles within departments over increases in statistics requirements, which were often resented by students, whose interests in sociology were substantive and sometimes practical or theoretical. They often failed to see the relevance of what were perceived to be onerous demands. Moreover, the faculty members who did not conform to these new standards rebelled against them, sometimes effectively, often at the cost of departmental harmony. The most ardent advocates of statistical methods were in several cases involved in particularly brutal efforts to eliminate the opposition and define it as "unprofessional" or incompetent.

The political struggles within departments contributed to disputes over the nature of social science and to the creation of a critical literature. Much of this critical literature centered on the notion of "positivism." There is a great irony here, because the antecedents of the faith in statistical methods as a road to science were not originally "positivist" in inspiration and because the standard arguments of the prominent "positivist" philosophers of the time, such as C. G. Hempel, could as readily be deployed against the atheoretical statistical work of the era as for it. In any case, as the critics soon discovered, there was a large body of "antipositivist" philosophical opinion outside of sociology that denied the "scientific" status of sociology. Moreover, for many sociologists concerned with specific substantive problems, the rise of quantitative methods was experienced as alien and external, escalating to a sense of alienation from the national discipline. Even sociologists who were well trained by the standards of the time found their skills rapidly becoming obsolete, with the literature of the most prestigious journals in their own field becoming inaccessible to them.

At the end of the 1950s, two traditions faced each other: the Fisherian tradition of demonstrating differences—paradigmatically differences in 2x2 tables—between random and nonrandom distributions, and a revived form of correlational analysis. Samuel Stouffer, in one of his last writings, described the recent history of the alternatives in this way:

> In the past decade or two there seems to have been a drift away from some of the conventional techniques, like correlation, in spite of some of their mathematical advantages. The tendency has been more in the direction of subdividing and resubdividing the data successfully as additional variables are introduced, often treating each variable as having only two or three broad categories. . . .
>
> There is another trend in analysis, however, which may lead in other directions. I refer to the increasing use of high-speed electronic computing machines, which are now readily available to behavioral scientists. Training in programming the new computers is now part of the experience which many of our graduate students are getting. One of these IBM monsters in an hour produces huge matrices of

correlation coefficients which might have taken a clerk with a desk calculator a year to do. (1963, pp. 74-75)

The first type of alternative was easy to produce: the technology required was the card-sorter and the calculator. As late as the mid-1960s departments had "statistics labs" that contained these devices, which students were expected to master and use in order to produce the dozens of tables that would make up the data presentation for a dissertation or research article. Students often collected their own data. Like psychology departments, sociology departments, which often shared a "social psychology" program, used the students in introductory courses as subjects for questionnaire studies. Other locally generated survey data, very often from a funded survey project on which a student had worked as an assistant, was available, and this material formed the subject matter for the typical dissertation, which tested some set of hypotheses, for example, null difference hyotheses on which a causal interpretation could be placed. The available data typically included demographic variables, which served as surrogate controls, as well as input and output variables that showed the consequences of some social variation. The explanatory variations, and sometimes the outputs, were often made up scales, based on questionnaire responses, of attitudinal properties such as religiosity, anomie, and the like.

Differences, which were conventionally treated as "significant" at the 0.05 level, were easy to find—as Paul Meehl has pointed out (1986). The null hypotheses that were being rejected in these "tests" were almost always known to be literally false, or reasonably expected to be false. The variables in question were obviously not distributed randomly either in relation to one another or to a large number of other, unmeasured or unincluded variables, and the higher the number of cases, the more likely it was that these relationships would be "significant." So a finding of a "difference" was of little value, unless, as was rarely the case in sociological projects, one had clear reasons to believe that one had identified precisely the only statistically and causally relevant variables. Not surprisingly, "results" proliferated.

The ready availability of funds for surveys, the ease of generating "results" using this kind of statistical method, the accessibility of the data, the loose measurement conventions, and the accessibility of the technology meant that the journal market for this kind of work was quickly flooded. In many areas of research, a great deal of faddism in statistical methods occurred. This faddism was aided by the fact that the persons who set the fads were able to preserve their leadership by setting them, whereas others in less central institutions had to invest their efforts in catching up, only to discover that their expensively acquired new skills were now outdated.

From the point of view of the competitive struggle for space in prestigious journals, other properties of the methods were also relevant. First, novel statistical methods were often not well described in the literature, and, consequently, access was initially limited to a few sociologists in a few departments. Second, the methods made most of the technical training of most practicing sociologists obsolete or obsolescent. In addition to the investment necessary to master the methods themselves, the user had to master the computer techniques necessary for the computations. Finally, the methods required, for their full use, more data than individuals could ordinarily collect without significant grant support.

This initially meant that the universities with access to significant funds for developing large bodies of data had an advantage over the less-well-equipped universities. But the main use of the methods turned out to be in secondary analysis of existing data, a development connected to various other trends, such as the general decline of experimental social psychology (as psychology departments were engulfed by their own "cognitive revolution") and the increasing cost of surveys.

The last development was decisive. The funding atmosphere for sociology changed radically as the Nixon presidency progressed in the 1970s, with the result that individual sociologists were compelled to rely on collectively generated data, such as the General Social Survey of the National Opinion Research Center. Not since the old Bureau of Statistics of Labor (Massachusetts) (see Chapter 1) had reliance on collectively generated data been so prevalent. The main means of competing under these new circumstances was not so much the collection of huge amounts of new data, but rather the refinement of techniques for analyzing existing data or data collected for other purposes. To succeed one needed methods of making distinctions that could not be made with ordinary structural equation methods, of compensating for missing values, and the like. And so these kinds of refinements became the preoccupation of the methodologists of the 1970s and 1980s (see Turner and Turner, n.d. for a review of these).

The monopoly of these methods is far from absolute, or, put differently, the valued methods of analysis do not form a cohesive whole. Variant methodological traditions, including a number of variant quantitative traditions, have survived or been founded in the period after the 1960s. Lazarsfeld believed Leo Goodman's revival of contingency table methods to be on the right path, and network analysis has produced a number of devices that have become briefly fashionable, such as the short-lived "block modeling" approach. Some work has been done with economic models, and The Journal of Mathematical Sociology has continued to publish work in formal methods. Of course, qualitative methods, such as participant observation, have also survived, albeit generally in the less prestigious reaches of the discipline.

CONCLUSION

In response to the sudden infusion of material resources—primarily post-Sputnik governmental funds and baby-boom students with heightened ideological concerns—American sociology grew rapidly. Such growth created pressures for reorganization of the profession, but the resulting expansion of the ASA did not involve an increase in either organizational control or intellectual coherence in the profession. Indeed, just the opposite appears to have ensued: ASA became an umbrella organization seeking to accommodate all viewpoints and all persons willing to pay dues. Moreover, the field rapidly differentiated outside of

ASA, as became evident by the increased number of journals, specialty associations, course offerings in departments, and separation of regional associations from ASA.

This diversity has reached the point where it is clear that American sociology has profound integrative problems. Such problems have always existed in sociology, as they do in all professions. But they have always been particularly severe in sociology, as we have tried to document in Chapters 1-3. Indeed, the current state of the discipline is the result of the failure of the early compromises to integrate the field, and when material resources greatly expanded in the modern era, there was no way to unify, either organizationally or symbolically, American sociology. Thus, the specific historical processes outlined in Chapters 1-3 created a set of conditions that, when dramatic growth occurred, pushed sociology in many different directions. Such has been the story of this chapter. Now we should ponder why this historical legacy, coupled with the current state of diversity, presents sociology with some difficult problems that make it "the impossible science."

FIVE

Possible Sociologies, Recalcitrant Worlds: Conclusion

From the time of the original compromises that made sociology into an academic discipline, conscious efforts by sociologists to change the discipline have varied in response to fluctuations in the available resources. Attempts to reform sociology have produced a number of ideal pictures of what sociology can, or should, be. Yet each has failed, and we can rightly ask why such has been the case. Each ideal model has had its own special obstacles to realization, but there are some underlying patterns in the failures and successes. In this concluding chapter we will consider a series of images of the discipline, all of which persist in one form or another today, but none of which has succeeded in establishing the resource base that could integrate sociology into a coherent discipline.

SOCIOLOGY AS THE GENERAL SOCIAL SCIENCE

Albion Small and Franklin Giddings saw sociology as having scientific possibilities, but neither treats these possibilities as the whole of the discipline. Indeed, they and their students created departments in which "applied" concerns had an important place. In particular, Giddings's students took a great interest in the uses of sociology and contributed to the literature on public welfare systems, and his students Howard Odum and F. Stuart Chapin built up schools of social work. They did so at a time when the discipline of social work was not well developed and when their distinctive professional identity as "sociologists" was not especially firm (Chapin began his teaching career as an economist, and W. F. Ogburn often identified himself as one). Ogburn's presidential address to the ASS in 1930 was an attempt to deal with some of the intellectual issues, but the relation of scientific sociology to social concerns was not addressed directly until after World War II, at a time when many sociologists were convinced that the field was on the verge of becoming a genuine science and required relief, at least temporarily, from demands for "solutions" to social problems.

Scientific purism was not without exponents in the interwar era, but the few examples indicate the difficulty of creating an institutional base. William Graham Sumner's student Albert Keller, who rejected the term "sociology" in favor of the phrase "science of society" and who never accepted the organizational authority of the American Sociological Society, represented an option which perhaps could have been viable only at a wealthy private university. Moreover, his views could only persist for the period before the large Ivy League universities became more heavily dependent on graduate education and on the production of disciplinary Ph.D.'s for an employment market defined by the expectations of a non-Ivy League Market. In the 1930s, Harvard under Sorokin stressed "theory" and especially the kind of comprehensive, overarching social theory that Keller had in mind, but at Harvard as well as elsewhere, the student audience for theoretical sociology of this sort was not large.

Limited as this Ivy League base was, it sufficed to support a number of figures and several movements that served the purpose of providing a nonpolitical and essentially elitist and anti-democratic ideology for young members of the American upper classes who felt the need for some kind of conception of their social role beyond what could be found in the populist and constitutionalist American political tradition. For example, the Pareto cult that developed at Harvard in the 1920s under the influence of the biologist L. J. Henderson sought to analyze society as a kind of patient in need of therapeutic control rather than political liberal leadership.

The idea of a purely scientific sociology, one devoted entirely to the "science of society," remained a *part* of sociology at many other universities, but with a few exceptions, it persisted as a small and difficult-to-assimilate part. At Chicago, where it had been represented by Albion Small, it survived in the teaching of sociologists like Louis Wirth and in the theory requirements for the Ph.D. And up to the present, doctoral programs in sociology require theory—the core of a science—but such a modest source of demand enabled theoretical purism to survive only in a dependent relation to the rest of the discipline, as it did in Small's time at Chicago. At the Chicago department in this era most students were more interested in reform or amelioration, and in the less-prestigious universities, the same pattern held: students with practical or reformist interests were the basic audience and resource, and "scientific" sociology survived only as a small component of a larger discipline that met different needs of its principle constituents.

SOCIOLOGY AS A REFORM DISCIPLINE

In 1903, Charles Ellwood, then 28, had taken a position at the University of Missouri. One of his first acts was to conduct a survey of the state's jails and poorhouses. He was widely criticized in the newspapers of the state for his report, and, as one newspaper columnist put it,

> there was great indignation and the professor was accused of slandering his state. One of the weekly newspapers declared that if a "nincompoop" wished to gain a little notoriety all he need do was to find fault with the people who were giving him his bread and butter. Others said that if

certain individuals did not like what they saw in Muzzoora there were plenty of roads leading out of that state, the inference being that the critics had better leave Muzzoora.

Ellwood continued to get into difficulties over his views, such as his remarks on the low level of local public morality in the wake of a lynching in the 1920s. Yet it was precisely these remarks including his prescient denunciations of Italian fascism in the early 1930s at a time when Mussolini was widely admired in the United States, that made sociology an attractive field of study for committed reformist students. Ellwood attracted many such students and maintained a lifelong connection with some of those who continued in social service careers.

The newspaper criticisms raised a crucial question about the viability of this model of critical sociology. Why would politicians allow the university to employ persons who set themselves up as authoritative critics of the society and, more particularly, of the political structure that employed them? In Ellwood's case, he survived the criticism in large part because of his visible Christian devotion. His close connection with the churches, his lecturing to them, and his "religious" writing produced the kind of edifying "sociology" that later sociologists dismissed as preaching. Such lectures protected him from his enemies, but this protection was for an individual rather than a discipline as a whole.

Thus the model of sociology as a reform discipline rested on some poorly institutionalized conditions, religious in Ellwood's case and political in the case of others, such as E. A. Ross. The career of Robert S. Lynd, who also formulated a conception of sociology as a reform discipline, reflected a somewhat different pattern of dependence. Lynd rose into the inner circles of the Rockefeller reformers as a liberal preacher who had published a number of articles critical of a Rockefeller mining community and who was then hired, at a very comfortable salary, as an employee of one of the organizations supported by Rockefeller funds. Lynd had no use for edification in the sense practiced by Charles Ellwood, for his "audience" was the group of liberal

Protestant New Yorkers of which Rockefeller's functionaries and the other members of the nascent foundation community were part. They were not populists, and their concern was not with enlightening the electorate. Rather, their interest was in social action as it could be induced and directed from the top. Lynd, like his mentor and ally Lawrence Frank, set himself up as a kind of social diagnostician and focused on the reform of American culture. But the performance of this role depended on the support of the community of foundation leaders and wealthy reformers. The lectures that became his famous *Knowledge for What?* ([1939] 1967) were delivered to just such an audience at Princeton University in 1938. Yet this was an exceptionally limited resource base, and it was to disappear as a result of imminent changes in the social character of the faculties and, to some extent, student bodies of the Ivy League universities.

Lynd's message was for people like Lynd himself—innocent but idealistic children of well-to-do Protestants who were able to spend their years at college "finding themselves" and coming to ideological terms with the larger reality of power in the society. The idea of "society as a patient" was not an uncompelling model. At Harvard, for example, the same imagery attracted the disciples of L. J. Henderson and Walter B. Cannon, including Parsons himself. But Lynd did not institutionalize this model into a successful means for attracting and transforming students, and by the 1940s the students who were taking Lynd's courses at Columbia were sophisticated ideologically and found him sympathetic but simplistic (Heeren, 1975, p. 207). More importantly, graduate students did not find in Lynd's teaching a set of problems that could be solved with the skills being imparted, and they could not see how Lynd's approach would enable them to make their way in the academic world. In contrast, emerging figures like Paul Lazarsfeld provided precisely these skills and the sense that such skills could be used to forge an academic career.

Nor did Lynd have a relevant image of sociology as an academic discipline. In *Knowledge for What?* he argued that sociology ought to give up its pretensions to being the general social science and become instead a collection of practical "problem areas." He argued that disciplines "conducted as internally self-perpetuating academic traditions" were obstacles to "the effective handling of the most fundamental cultural snarls." The lines between the disciplines, he hoped, would "blur" ([1939] 1967, pp. 167-168), but in so advocating, Lynd ignored the practical reality that most sociologists at the time were employed as teachers in the business of perpetuating an academic tradition. They were not well-connected foundation luminaries like Lynd.

Lynd's naiveté and isolation aside, the idea of sociology as a critical discipline has nevertheless had a long and consequential afterlife. In the hands of C. Wright Mills, for example, the critical approach became a ghost that haunted American sociology. The power of the idea rested on a crucial resource: undergraduate students disaffected with contemporary social life. In the 1960s, when such students were attracted to sociology and to the sociologists who gave voice to their concerns, the discipline experienced its greatest growth. When the student movement receded, the quantity and quality of students declined precipitously. The "radical" sociology that subsequently emerged was now protected by well-established conventions of academic freedom. Yet, in contrast to the 1960s, the student market for radical approaches was small. The radicals themselves reacted in various ways: some became increasingly philosophical, others became relentless careerists whose radicalism was largely nominal. But the reformist impulse that has always been a part of American sociology persisted in new forms, such as "practical" sociology or, as it is often called today, "sociological practice."

SOCIOLOGY AS PRACTICAL EXPERTISE

A variant to the model of sociology as a kind of policy science is sociology as a profession. In the course of the dispute over the overproduction of Ph.D.'s in sociology during the 1930s, F. Stuart Chapin (1934) who assumed that the Ph.D. degree was properly awarded only to persons who were to hold university positions, was countered by the chairman of the department at Chicago,

Ellsworth Faris, who argued that "sociology as a subject merely to be taught is a parasite." Instead, Faris envisioned an "increase in the demand for men of sociological training in research and administration in government departments," in high school teaching and administration, and in rural areas as county agents (1934a, pp. 511-512). Some Chicago graduates of the era did pursue careers in official statistics, but no great increase in demand for such skills occurred. The sheer diversity of Faris's list is revealing, for there was no clear location in an organizational or professional system for someone with an academic background in sociology.

The idea of sociological practice, however, has deep roots in the sociological tradition. The original aims of Wardian sociology were to provide the intellectual framework for a telic sociology, and the notion of social telesis as a distinctive province of sociology has survived in various forms throughout its history. For instance, Giddings included a chapter on the subject in his methods book of the 1920s, and his student Herbert Shenton did a dissertation on telesis in the same period. And throughout the discipline, sociologists were involved in discussions of public welfare and in what today would be called "comparative welfare systems." Chicago was exceptional in its lack of a close relationship between its sociology department and the School of Social Welfare, whereas North Carolina and Minnesota, under Odum and Chapin respectively, started schools of social welfare. Yet, in time, the task of training social workers for practice in agencies led to distinctive professional orientation that had less and less to do with sociology and more to do with the business of psychotherapy or counseling, which was extremely attractive as a career to many persons and which could provide skills that were in great demand. But these were not skills that sociologists were prepared to impart, or acquire.

The fact that sociologists were so heavily involved during the formation of social work as a professional discipline diminished their sense that they should create a separate professional niche for themselves. Faris's suggestion that sociologists might become county agents provides additional evidence of the problems found by sociologists in finding a "practical" niche for themselves in the "real world." Rural sociologists were active in training workers who participated in the extension services, and, indeed, the "extension sociologist" became a professional category within the structure of agricultural programs of land grant universities. But the category was not large, and the sheer diversity of the kinds of applied work that sociologists ultimately did perform, such as marriage counseling, penology, and organizational development consulting, meant that the category "sociologist" in itself could not signal much about the relevant preparation of the individual bearer of this title.

In the 1930s, under the pressure of the difficult academic job market and the crisis of the Depression, efforts to more fully realize the potential of sociology in the formation of policy expanded, and a serious attempt was made to establish a distinct place for sociologists within government bureaucratic structures. The lessons of "planning" as practiced in fascist Italy, Nazi Germany, and Stalinist Russia were discussed at length in the early issues of the *American Sociological Review*. Yet the reports on the experiences of sociology departments that had made determined efforts to participate in planning activities during the Depression were not encouraging. Philip A. Parsons, a student of Giddings who was professor of sociology at the University of Oregon, reported on a particularly serious attempt to involve the sociology department with the work of the state planning board, primarily by conducting "needs assessment" surveys supported by a substantial grant. The effort was modeled on the successful efforts of political scientists to participate in public policy, but Parsons's list of the obstacles faced by this effort is daunting: resistance came from the "exponents of . . . traditional charity"; from "the unlettered," who objected to "highbrows" and pitted the sociologists and social workers against legislators, businessmen, and county judges and "who felt themselves to be 'practical' and the sociologists 'theoretical' "; and from defenders of the status quo, who feared the results of research (1936, p. 368).

The same kind of list could be generated in connection with other attempts to influence "policy." The antagonists were interested parties, often with well-developed views of the problems on which policy was being made. The idea that they would abdicate these interests in favor of the pronouncements of sociologists was unrealistic. Yet sociologists who were personally suited to the politics of policy, such as Carroll Wright, William F. Ogburn, and later James S. Coleman, played important roles in public life and used their professional skills as researchers to affect policy outcomes. They did not, however, institutionalize a role that other, less politically adept sociologists could fill after them. The bulk of the sociologists who served in governmental posts were no more than "bureaucratic technicians" (Merton and Lerner, 1951) whose contribution was in the conduct of research rather than in the thinking that produced policy.

The reasons behind this failure lie as much in the peculiarities of "policy"-making processes itself as in the failings of sociology. These peculiarities have been well described by various authors, including sociologists such as Amitai Etzioni (1967). Their message, which has been applied to the uses of the hard sciences in policy by such writers as Collingridge and Reeve (1986), is that policy is made by learning about the unintended consequences with incremental adjustments to existing policies in an atmosphere of uncertainty, particularly the unexpected political consequences of past decisions. The role of "science," "policy science," or "sociology" in these adjustments is necessarily limited. This role does not involve "planning" or conceptualizing, much less providing empirical justifications for particular policy solutions. In short, policy is of necessity largely "cut and try," and sociologists can contribute to this process only to the extent that they can facilitate it. And they can ordinarily facilitate policy only in limited ways, such as providing evaluations on effects of policies. However, those sociologists who attempted to make a business of evaluation research soon learned in the 1970s that they were servants of clients who had an interest in the outcomes of the evaluations conducted for them, an interest which they were quite able to enforce by declining to employ researchers who failed to prove the desired effects, or lack of effect. In any event, the demand for this kind of work was limited, and the competition for it from practitioners of other disciplines was intense. As a result, policy research and "sociological practice," as this whole area is now called, could not secure a sufficiently large or stable resource base to redirect sociology.

THE POSTWAR SYNTHESIS

The idea of "making sociology into a science" that developed in the post-World War II era itself contained the seeds of a reconciliation of the diverse elements of sociology. The key to this reconciliation was the dramatic attempt to integrate theory and research in a way that went beyond the "pure science" approach of the early generation (see earlier discussion). The ambitious proposals of the era—particularly Parsons's overarching conceptual schemes and Merton's strategic emphasis on the middle ground between theory and research—were made in an attempt to integrate diversity. The process of integration had prior roots, of course. For example, the Sociological Research Association in the 1930s attempted to involve "theorists" who were either politically indispensable or congenial. Both Parsons and Merton fell into this category, but both were representatives of Harvard's almost exclusively "theoretical" orientation, and neither was linked to the dominant empirical tradition represented by the students of Giddings. Yet both attempted to make their peace with empirical sociology. Parsons did so by establishing a relationship with Samuel Stouffer, then the leading Chicago statistical sociologist and the leading figure in the generation of statistical sociologists trained by Giddings's students, William F. Ogburn, F. Stuart Chapin, and Howard Odum. Merton did so by establishing a close personal bond with Paul Lazarsfeld.

There never was a single, clear, consensual model of the new sociology, and many of the accommodations were superficial. Nevertheless, a highly persuasive general image of the scientific future of the discipline did emerge. Parsons made his own theory conform to the common understanding of science by the device of treating it as a preliminary to a positive, physicslike "theory."

Merton and Stouffer had somewhat different views, but each emphasized the idea of small-scale theories that would serve as part of a more complete future theory. Lazarsfeld was more skeptical than Merton about the prospects for general theory, for he believed that the complexities of social life precluded any kind of theory beyond the level of social psychology. Social psychology was thus to become the tactical common ground for Merton and Lazarsfeld as well as for the foundations over which they had influence and, to some extent, for the discipline as a whole. In several ways, it was a peculiarly powerful integrating idea. The concern of such figures as Lynd with "culture" could be treated as potentially explicable by social psychology, particularly socialization and group influences on the individual. And concepts from the classical tradition could be restated in social psychological terms, though sometimes with strange results, as in the case of Merton's reformulation of the concept of anomie (Besnard, 1986, 1987). But despite the problems that were to reduce the influence of social psychology in American sociology, the reformulations of the 1950s and early 1960s acquired a certain plausibility because they could be used to construct hypotheses that successfully predicted. The "tests" were of course very weak, and the hope of transforming these hypotheses into something actually resembling physics was of course distant. But the successes served as a kind of down payment on the promises made to the foundations that a significant concentration on basic theory and methods in sociology would potentially produce a breakthrough. With this persuasive image, the "mainstream" of American sociology was established.

The persons who were persuaded included the community of foundation officers in New York, and the decisive initial advantage of this new "mainstream" of sociology over its potential competitors was a consequence of foundation support. In time, when the funds diminished and when other material resources like student demand increased, mainstream sociology lost its relative advantage. The advantage of mainstream "theory" was lost first, whereas mainstream "quantitative methods" had a broader resource base and greater access to funds for research related to government social aims. But Lazarsfeld-style survey sociology also faltered in the 1970s in favor of cheaper methods, with roots in interwar statistical sociology, that could be used for analysis of existing data.[1] The fact that these methods were applied most successfully by persons with access to the more stable but less munificent funding sources was perhaps crucial as well. Yet the *relative* advantage of "mainstream" quantitative research methods against heterodox sociologies has lasted into the present, because of the *relative* ease with which research projects can serve both sociological and administrative aims. Nevertheless, the present situation stands in sharp contrast to the period in which the foundations believed that they were making sociology a "science" by their funding of theory-research projects. Such beliefs are not typical of the current generation of quantitative researchers, much less of their sources of financial support.

In "resource" and institutional terms, the new sociology "as a science" was an extraordinary ambitious construction. This construction involved not just external funding, but appeals to traditional student audiences as well. The intellectual leadership of sociology worked very successfully at creating an appropriate literature for undergraduate students. In particular, Merton produced a social problems text and a highly researchable explanation of crime. Thus there was no sense in which the traditional audience of socially concerned students was being abandoned in favor of a Keller-like purism of the earlier period to make sociology a "pure science." The policy relevance of sociology was also being asserted, and research into the great problems of American life, notably race, continued. Moreover, new practical domains, notably medicine, were colonized with considerable success (behavioral science programs were established in many medical schools during this period). In essence, the new model combined the best of the past models. It had the advantages of reform sociology, without the political risks of public edification of the variety practiced by Ellwood, Ross, or Harry Elmer Barnes. It had the advantages of a profession, by virtue of its place in professional schools, without the creation of a specific occupational category. And for the first time in sociology's history in America, this quest for a scientific sociology became the core of departmental life in all the major sociology programs.

The initial successes of the model with student audiences, foundations, and professional schools concealed difficulties that became apparent in time. The first difficulty was the need, endlessly reiterated in the literature of the late 1940s and 1950s, for a particular kind of "theory" that would be simultaneously scientific and useful. This was an old problem, exemplified in the ambiguous desire of the Rockefeller patrons of social science in the 1920s for "realistic studies." From the point of view of the foundations, it was not solved in the 1950s, and so support was withdrawn. For example, the Ford Foundation, which had supported the idea of social psychology very generously, ultimately concluded that the effort was unsuccessful and cut off funds. Although new funding replaced the old, support for research without immediate practical value diminished—dramatically so in the Nixon years. The idea of a practically useful form of theory was perhaps simply premature, but it was the centerpiece of the new model. Analogous difficulties arose in connection with survey research, where the conflict between "sociologically interesting" and fundable work was often severe.

Although the well-funded work done by Parsons, Stouffer, Merton, and Lazarsfeld set the standard in the late 1940s, 1950s, and early 1960s, it was possible for alternative forms of research and theory to develop and establish a sufficient resource base to survive. In particular, the ideas of mainstream sociology that were applied to specific areas, such as complex organizations, soon were faced with competitors, often tailored more closely to specific purposes, such as management training. Within sociology, similar kinds of competition developed. Alternative theories or approaches to specific domains or problems were proposed and often developed into distinctive schools of thought. The expansion of the 1960s diminished the relative advantages of the major departments in placing students, and as a result new centers of thinking could develop. Moreover, the new demand for research activity on the part of sociologists in institutions that were once solely teaching institutions meant that graduates of minor or peripheral programs were more likely to produce research. Thus alternative approaches could sustain themselves, modestly, as minor academic traditions. These "sustainable rebellions" are the main political feature of present sociology.

Why did they emerge, and how did they sustain themselves? In the first stage of the new consensual order, during the interwar years, the lead was taken by such persons as Chapin, whereas in the second stage, after 1945, it was assumed by the theorists Parsons and Merton. For reasons intrinsic to the methodological and theoretical heritage of Giddings's sociology, which was itself based on "the problem of order," the legitimacy of this kind of direction was accepted, at least temporarily. Odum, for instance, became one of the more enthusiastic purveyors of the new model. From the point of view of this older generation, the younger sociologists to whom the baton was being passed were taking up their task. The generational bonds were personal as well: Stouffer revered Ogburn, his former teacher, and was admired by Ogburn's generation.

But the consensus was both extremely limited and extremely tenuous. Many of the sociologists who were part of what may broadly be called the reform tradition were unwilling to accept one central premise of the new order: the idea of an uncommitted sociology. The founding of the Society for the Study of Social Problems in 1953 was the first important institutional manifestation of the process of alliance creation within the groups of sociologists excluded from the new order. It was not the last, and it showed that rebellion was sustainable, even in the hard times of the mid-1950s. Why was it sustainable? The great shift of the era was from legitimacy granted by the publication of authoritative textbooks to a legitimacy granted by the publication of articles in professional journals. This was largely an external shift, resulting from changes in larger patterns of academic communication. The rebels—in this case, rebels of what in retrospect was a very modest rebellion—established a new journal, *Social Problems*, which, in the face of the dearth of publication opportunities in the era, soon enjoyed a large readership and a respectable set of contributors, including many students of those who had forged the new consensus.

Social Problems was a significant precedent. In the 1960s, the society that sponsored it became a haven for rebels of various kinds, but, perhaps more importantly, it served as a monument to the possibility of rejecting tenets of the new order. Many more monuments were soon to be constructed, especially in the 1960s, when they could be based on student demand at the graduate level. The precedent has been repeated many times over, creating a situation of fragmentation in the wake of the fleeting consensus of the post-World War II period.

When enrollments and funding collapsed in the 1970s, mainstream sociology was affected as severely as the heterodoxies that had established an academic base. But the forms of sociology that survived the contraction of the 1970s and 1980s were diverse, and the constraints of funding led to even greater diversity. Particular heterodox traditions, such as symbolic interactionism, successfully established their own journals, societies, and awards structure, while attracting just enough students to continue to produce Ph.D.'s and place them in academic positions. The resource needs of the forms of sociology that survive under present circumstances are few. In the case of symbolic interactionism, this resource base is associated with teaching a popular set of courses, with student demand for these courses being sufficient to sustain a modest demand for new instructors. Other heterodox traditions have managed to survive in other ways. Some ethnomethodologists, for example, have found employment in departments of communication, an expanding academic field. The existence of these alternatives has meant that the constraints of membership in the discipline of sociology are, in several respects, diminishing as a de facto fulfillment of Lynd's hope for a blurring of disciplinary lines. Many of the academic opportunities for sociologists are in new kinds of departments, such as Criminal Justice and Science and Technology Studies programs. The ability of sociologists to leave sociology departments and join the new academic communities that have grown up around these programs frees them from the few avenues of social control that the discipline still exercises. Freedom to ignore the discipline's journals and avoid the editorial constraints of the "prestigious" journals of the discipline is decisive, for this source of control is essential to the coherence of an intellectual community, and it is the key to most other constraints.

CONCLUSION: SOCIOLOGY FOR WHOM?

The major resource for present sociology is undergraduate students. The important graduate departments are at the top of a great food chain: undergraduate demand feeds demand for graduate students at the lesser universities, and graduate demand at the lesser universities feeds demand for graduate students at the major departments. The decline in this basic resource has implications for the whole chain. Some departments have been able to find substitutes for dependence on this chain, particularly third world students. In a very few cases, sociologists have found alternative funding sources for research that reduce their dependence on this chain. But the chain remains fundamental to the support of most sociologists. Yet the competition for undergraduate students has never been so intense, and the relative value of a liberal arts degree has diminished as a consequence of competition with programs that can promise employment opportunities. Sociology departments in many universities have been reduced to the role of providing "service courses" for majors in other, more vocationally oriented programs. But unlike economics, which provides many courses that are required for business students, sociology ordinarily has only a small mandated role in the curricula of other fields, and there it must compete for students by providing courses for general education requirements that can be met by courses in other departments.

The availability of problem-oriented academic programs and courses means that the traditional process by which sociology attracted students and transformed them can no longer easily operate. Few undergraduate students have any interest in the "theoretical" or "methodological" issues of pure sociology, or sociology understood as a pure science. As in the past, the typical undergraduate student of today is attracted to sociology because of the topics sociologists study, particularly crime, juvenile delinquency, family problems, and the like. However, these topics may be found in a half-dozen other departments these days, and so sociology has lost much of its "monopoly" on social problems and human misery.

There are few alternatives for sociology besides this ever more fragmented audience, and some of the past alternatives have disappeared. For example, a small group of students exists that is sufficiently well educated or possesses the general culture to be interested in the challenge sociology poses to the political or religious frames of reference in which they were raised. But this ideological need, which was perhaps met by such teachers as Giddings, is no longer as powerful as it once was and cannot serve to motivate a significant number of students.

It is perhaps not surprising that the students who took the place of the rebels against Presbyterian orthodoxy of the early years of American sociology were the children of immigrants, persons who were undergoing their own ordeals of civility and secularity. Other social changes had similar effects. The end of the massive immigration before the First World War meant that this population group too would disappear. The diminished centrality of the problem of race in the lives of educated southerners meant that this source of sociologists was also going to dry up. Other audiences for sociology as a purely intellectual discipline have disappeared as well. Several of Giddings's students held teaching posts at exclusive women's colleges, and they dominated Smith. In the interwar years, these colleges sought to produce socially concerned and politically conscious graduates who were expected to marry wealth and use their leisure for the public good. Changes in opportunities and expectations for women gradually undermined this model. The audience of the 1960s that inspired fear and loathing among the sociological establishment disappeared on its own. But the 1960s transformed some disciplines—notably American studies, English, history, and, to some extent, political science—in ways that made them formidable competitors for the diminished audience of politically radical students, thereby decreasing yet another constituency of sociology.

When Lynd treated sociology as the residual social science, concerned with a hodgepodge of topics, this characterization was particularly true of the undergraduate level of work. In the past, as Lynd saw, this was a source of demand, but at present, when the size of this residual space has been reduced as a result of competition with new programs, the failure of sociology thus far to establish a "professional" role or a close alliance with a strong profession has been devastating. Without bonds like those of political science with law and public administration or economics with business, sociology is vulnerable as specialized programs ally themselves more closely with particular sectors formerly served by sociology and, in the process, provide much of the competition for the resources that student bodies generate in American academia.

Thus the conditions under which American sociology initially expanded have disappeared. The discipline is now driven cognitively by the logic of its own internal competition for prestige and consequently has changed in ways that make it less likely than before to serve the intellectual needs of large audiences in American culture. Perhaps sociologists will find some manner in which they can market their skills to "clients" outside the academic world. But the market in which they must do so is uncongenial, although at the moment we write these words sociology enrollments are on the upswing. Many of the skills have become generic—for example, the typical graduate student in a professional business program is likely to get a more advanced and demanding training in which was formerly known as "social statistics" than are Ph.D. sociologists. And many of the activities formerly performed by "expert" quantitative sociologists and demographers are now performed by user-friendly demographic computer programs devised to serve the specialized needs of marketing specialists and advertising agencies. These problems, however, exist for the profession as a whole, at a time when the collective powers of the profession, always modest, are at a low ebb.

Under these conditions, the preferred strategy of the individual sociologist is to become a member of a sustaining academic school, with access to respectable journals, funding agencies, and markets for teachers. The choices of individuals in the face of the constraints of their immediate environments are decisive. For unless new audiences and, hence, new resource bases can be found, these constraints will seem so severe as to eliminate sociology as a realm in which individuals make choices. Sociology will, of course, continue to exist in some form—most likely as a collection of loosely integrated topics and subfields. But the hopes of the founding compromise, as it has been periodically resurrected, for a scientific sociology are increasingly remote and unconstraining on individual students and sociologists as they make career choices. Either the practical conditions for the intellectual ambitions of the discipline or the intellectual conditions for the practical institutional ambitions of the discipline have remained tantalizingly close but out of reach. These conditions are entrenched. And so, while sociology may always exist, and perhaps prosper in periods of high student interest, it will remain the impossible science.

NOTE

1. It is striking that it was students of Ogburn and Chapin respectively, O. D. Duncan and William Sewell, who pioneered the application of path-analytic methods, methods that dealt with problems of interpreting partial correlations that had puzzled statistical sociologists from the late 1920s (see, for example, Duncan, 1966; Duncan, Featherman, and Duncan, 1972; Sewell and Hauser, 1975).

References

Aberle, D. F., A. K. Cohen, F. Davis, M. J. Levy, and F. X. Sutton. 1950. "The Functional Requisites of a Society." *Ethics* 55(January):100-111.

Abir-Am, Pnina G. 1987. "The Biotheoretical Gathering, Trans-Disciplinary Authority and the Incipient Legitimation of Molecular Biology in the 1930s: New Perspectives on the Historical Sociology of Science." *History of Science* 25:1-70.

Adler, Mortimer J. 1977. *Philosopher at Large: An Intellectual Autobiography*. New York: Macmillan.

Adorno, T. W., Else Frenkel-Brunswik, D. J. Levinson, and R. N. Sanford. 1950. *The Authoritarian Personality*. New York: Harper.

Alexander, Jeffrey C. 1982-1984. *Theoretical Logic in Sociology*, 4 vol. Berkeley: University of California Press.

Alexander, Jeffrey C. 1988. "General Theory in the Post Positivist Mode: The Epistemological Dilemma and the Search for Present Reason." Paper delivered at the Albany Conference, April 1988.

Bain, Read. 1927. "Trends in American Sociology." *Social Forces* 5 (1):413-422.

Bannister, Robert C. 1979. *Social Darwinism: Science and Myth in Anglo-American Social Thought*. Philadelphia: Temple University Press.

Bannister, Robert C. 1987. *Sociology and Scientism: The American Quest for Objectivity, 1880-1940*. Chapel Hill: University of North Carolina Press.

Bannister, Robert C. In press. "Principle, Politics, Profession: American Sociologists and Fascism, 1930-1950." In *Sociology Responds to Fascism*, edited by Dirk Kaesler and Stephen Turner. London: Routledge.

Barnes, Harry E. 1925. *The New History and the Social Studies*. New York: Century.

Barnes, Harry E. 1942. *The American Way of Life: Our Institutional Patterns and Social Problems*. Englewood Cliffs, NJ: Prentice-Hall.

Barnes, Harry E. 1948. *An Introduction to the History of Sociology*. Chicago: University of Chicago Press.

Barnes, Harry E. and Howard Becker. 1938. *Social Thought from Lore to Science*. Boston: D. C. Heath.

Barton, Allen H. 1982. "Paul Lazarsfeld and the Invention of the University Institute for Applied Social Research." In *Organizing for Social Research*, edited by Burkart Holzner and Jiri Nehnevajsa. Cambridge, MA: Schenkman.

Beard, Charles A. 1934. *The Nature of the Social Sciences in Relation to Objectives of Instruction*. New York: Scribner.

Bemis, Edward W. 1888. *Cooperation in the Middle States*. Johns Hopkins University Studies in Historical and Political Science, edited by Herbert B. Adams, Sixth Series III. Baltimore: Johns Hopkins University. (Reprint edition, 1973. New York: Johnson.)

Berelson, Bernard and Gary A. Steiner. 1964. *Human Behavior: An Inventory of Scientific Findings*. New York: Harcourt, Brace & World.

Bernard, Jessie. 1929. "The History and Prospects of Sociology in the United States." Pp. 1-71 in *Trends in American Sociology*, edited by George A. Lundberg, Read Bain, and Nels Anderson. New York: Harper & Brothers.

Bernard, L. L. 1928. "Some Historical and Recent Trends of Sociology in the United States." *Southwestern Political and Social Science Quarterly*, 9(2):264-293.

Bernard, L. L. 1924. *Instinct: A Study in Social Psychology*. New York: Holt.

Bernard, L. L. 1945. "The Teaching of Sociology in the United States in the Last Fifty Years." *American Journal of Sociology* 50(May):534-548.

Bernard, L. L. and Jessie Bernard. 1965. *Origins of American Sociology: The Social Science Movement in the United States*. New York: Russell & Russell.

Besnard, Philippe. 1986. "The Americanization of Anomie at Harvard." *Harvard and Society: Studies in the Sociology of Culture Past and Present* 6:41-53.

Besnard, Philippe. 1987. *L'anomie: Ses usages et ses fonctions dans la discipline sociologique depuis Durkheim*. Paris: Universitaires de France.

Bierstedt, Robert. 1981. *American Sociological Theory: A Critical History*. New York: Academic Press.

Black, Max. 1961. *The Social Theories of Talcott Parsons*. Englewood Cliffs, NJ: Prentice-Hall.

Blau, Peter M. 1964. *Exchange and Power in Social Life*. New York: Wiley.

Blau, Peter M. 1977. *Inequality and Heterogeneity, A Primitive Theory of Social Structure*. New York: The Free Press.

Blau, Peter M. and Otis D. Duncan. 1967. *The American Occupational Structure*. New York: Wiley.

Bliss, William D. P. 1898. *The Encyclopedia of Social Reforms*, 2nd ed. New York: Funk & Wagnalls.

Blumer, Herbert. 1939. "Critiques of Research in the Social Sciences I: An Appraisal of Thomas and Znaniecki's *The Polish Peasant in Europe and America*." New York: Social Science Research Council.

Blumer, Herbert. 1969. *Symbolic Interactionism*. Englewood Cliffs, NJ: Prentice-Hall.

Bogardus, Emory S. 1968. *The Development of Social Thought*, 4th ed. New York: David McKay.

Bromley, David G. and Frank J. Weed. 1979. "The Vanishing Sociology-Social Work Alliance: A Study in the Politics of Professionalism." *Journal of Sociology and Social Welfare* 5:168-187.

Brunner, Edmund de S., Gwendolyn S. Hughes, and Marjorie Patten. 1927. *American Agricultural Villages*. New York: George H. Doran.

Bulmer, Martin. 1984. *The Chicago School of Sociology: Institutionalization, Diversity, and the Rise of Sociological Research*. Chicago: University of Chicago Press.

Bureau of Statistics of Labor (Massachusetts). 1870. Report (I).

Bureau of Statistics of Labor (Massachusetts). 1872. Third Annual Report.

Bureau of Statistics of Labor (Massachusetts). 1874. Fifth Annual Report.

Buxton, William. 1985. *Talcott Parsons and the Capitalist Nation-State: Political Sociology as a Strategic Vocation*. Toronto: University of Toronto Press.

Buxton, William. 1989. "From National Morale to Social Control: The Wartime Origins of the Department of Social Relations at Harvard." Paper presented at Cheiron Meetings, June.

Buxton, William and Stephen Turner. 1990. "Edification and Expertise: Sociology as a Profession." In *Sociology and Its Publics*, edited by Terence C. Halliday and Morris Janowitz. Chicago: University of Chicago Press.

Camic, Charles. 1979. "The Utilitarians Revisited." *American Journal of Sociology* 85:516-550.

Chapin, F. Stuart. 1911. *Education and the Mores: A Sociological Essay*. New York: Columbia University, Longmans Green.

Chapin, Stuart F. 1920. *Field Work and Social Research*. New York: Century.

Chapin, F. Stuart. 1928. *Cultural Change*. New York: Century.

Chapin, F. Stuart. 1934. "The Present State of the Profession." *American Journal of Sociology* 39:506-508.

Clowse, Barbara Barksdale. 1981. *Brainpower for the Cold War: The Sputnik Crisis and National Defense Education Act of 1958*. Westport, CT: Greenwood Press.

Coleman, James S. 1987. "The Role of Social Policy Research in Society and Sociology." *The American Sociologist* 18(2):127-133.

Collingridge, David and Colin Reeve. 1986. *Science Speaks to Power: The Role of Experts in Policy Making*. New York: St. Martin's Press.

Collins, Randall. 1975. *Conflict Sociology*. New York: Academic Press.

Collins, Randall. 1984. "Statistics versus Words." *Sociological Theory* 2:329-362.

Comte, August. 1830-1842. *The Course of Positive Philosophy*. London: Bell & Sons.

Converse, Jean. 1987. *Survey Research in the United States: Roots and Emergence 1890-1960*. Berkeley: University of California Press.

Cooley, Charles Horton. 1902. *Human Nature and the Social Order*. New York: Scribner.

Cooley, Charles Horton. 1909. *Social Organization*. New York: Scribner.

Cooley, Charles Horton. 1918. *Social Process*. New York: Scribner.

Cressey, Paul G. 1932. *The Taxi-Dance Hall: A Sociological Study in Commercialized Recreation and City Life*. Chicago: University of Chicago Press.

Cross, Stephen J. and William R. Albury. 1987. "Walter B. Cannon, L. J. Henderson, and the Organic Analogy." *OSIRIS*, 2nd series 3:165-192.

Dahrendorf, Ralf. 1958. "Out of Utopia: Toward a Reorientation of Sociological Analysis." *American Journal of Sociology* 74(September):115-127.

Davis, Jerome and Harry E. Barnes. 1931. *An Introduction to Sociology*, rev. ed. Boston: D. C. Heath.

Davis, Kingsley. 1948. *Human Society*. New York: Macmillan.

Davis, Kingsley. 1959. "The Myth of Functional Analysis in Sociology and Anthropology." *American Sociological Review* 24:756-772.

Davis, Kingsley and Wilbert Moore. 1945. "Some Principles of Stratification." *American Sociological Review* 4:431-442.

Davis, Robert C. 1972. "Social Research in America before the Civil War." *Journal of the History of the Behavioral Sciences* 8:69-85.

Devine, Edward T. 1939. *When Social Work Was Young*. New York: Macmillan.

Diamond, Sigmund. 1963. "Some Early Uses of the Questionnaire." *Public Opinion Quarterly* 27:531-539.

Dibble, Vernon K. 1975. *The Legacy of Albion Small*. Chicago: University of Chicago Press.

Duncan, Otis Dudley. 1966. "Path Analysis: Sociological Examples." *American Journal of Sociology* 72:1-16.

Duncan, Otis Dudley, David Featherman, and Beverly Duncan. 1972. *Socioeconomic Background and Achievement*. New York: Seminar.

Durkheim, Émile. [1893] 1933. *The Division of Labor in Society*. New York: Macmillan.

Durkheim, Émile. [1912] 1915. *Elementary Forms of Religious Life*. New York: Macmillan.

Durkheim, Émile and Marcel Mauss. [1906] 1963. *Primitive Classification*. Chicago: University of Chicago Press.

Eaton, Allen and Shelby, M. Harrison. 1930. *A Bibliography of Social Surveys*. New York: Russell Sage Foundation.

Editor. 1880. "Editorial Page." *The Popular Science Monthly* 15(June):2.

Ellwood, Charles A. 1933. *Methods in Sociology: A Critical Study*. Durham, NC: Duke University Press.

Ellwood, Charles A. 1938. *A History of Social Philosophy*. Englewood Cliffs, NJ: Prentice-Hall.

Etzioni, Amatai. 1967. "Mixed-Scanning: A 'Third' Approach to Decision-Making." *Public Administration Review* 27(December):385-392

Etzkowitz, Henry. 1988. "The Contradictions of Radical Sociology." *Critical Sociology* 15:95-113.

Eubank, Earle E. 1932. *The Concepts of Sociology: A Treatise Presenting a Suggested Organization of Sociological Theory in Terms of Its Major Concepts*. Boston: D. C. Heath.

Faris, Ellsworth. 1934a. "Too Many Ph.D.'s?" *American Journal of Sociology* 39: 509-512.

Faris, Ellsworth. 1934b. "Review of *Methods of Sociology*." *American Journal of Sociology* 39:686-689.

Ferriss, Abbot L. 1964. "Sociological Manpower." *American Sociological Review* 29(February):103-114.

Fisher, Galen M. 1934. *The Institute for Social and Religious Research, 1921-1934*. New York.

Fones-Wolf, Kenneth. 1980. "Class, Professionalism and the Early Bureaus of Labor Statistics." *The Insurgent Sociologist* 10:38-45.

Ford Foundation. 1949. *Report of the Study for the Ford Foundation on Policy and Program*. Detroit: The Ford Foundation.

Fosdick, Raymond B. 1952. *The Story of the Rockefeller Foundation*. New York: Harper & Brothers.

Foskett, John M. 1949, "The Frame of Reference of Ward's Dynamic Sociology." *Research Studies, State College of Washington* 17:35-40.

Fox, Daniel M. 1967. *The Discovery of Abundance: Simon N. Patten and the Transformation of Social Theory*. Ithaca, NY: Cornell University Press.

Fox, Richard W. 1983. "Epitaph for Middletown: Robert S. Lynd and the Analysis of Consumer Culture." Pp. 103-141 in *The Culture of Consumption: Critical Essays in American History, 1880-1980*, edited by Richard W. Fox and J. J. Jackson. New York: Pantheon Books.

Fry, C. Luther. 1924. *Diagnosing the Rural Church: A Study in Method*. New York: George H. Doran.

Fuchs, Stephan and Jonathan H. Turner. 1986. "What Makes a Science Mature: Organizational Control in Scientific Production." *Sociological Theory* 4(7):143-150.

Furner, Mary O. 1975. *Advocacy and Objectivity: A Crisis in the Professionalization of American Social Science*. Lexington: University Press of Kentucky.

Galpin, Charles Josiah. 1920. *Rural Life*. New York: Century.

Galpin, Charles Josiah. 1938. *My Drift into Rural Sociology*. Baton Rouge: Louisiana State University Press.

Geiger, Roger L. 1986. *To Advance Knowledge: The Growth of American Research Universities, 1900-1940*. New York: Oxford University Press.

Giddens, Anthony. 1984. *The Constitution of Society*. Berkeley, CA: University of California Press.

Giddings, Franklin H. 1887. "The Theory of Profit-Sharing." *Quarterly Journal of Economics* 1:367-376.

Giddings, Franklin H. 1896. *The Principles of Sociology*. New York: Macmillan.

Giddings, Franklin H. 1901. *Inductive Sociology: A Syllabus of Methods, Analyses and Classifications, and Provisionally Formulated Laws*. New York: Macmillan.

Giddings, Franklin H. 1906. *Readings in Descriptive and Historical Sociology*. New York: Macmillan.

Giddings, Franklin H. 1920. *The Principles of Sociology: An Analysis of the Phenomena of Association and of Social Organization*, 3rd ed. New York: Macmillan.

Giddings, Franklin H. 1922. *Studies in the Theory of Human Society*. New York: Macmillan.

Giddings, Franklin H. 1924a. "Foreword." P. v in C. Luther Fry, *Diagnosing the Rural Church: A Study in Method*. New York: George H. Doran.

Giddings, Franklin H. 1924b 1974. *The Scientific Study of Human Society*. New York: Arno Press. (Reprint edition of 1924, Chapel Hill, University of North Carolina Press.)

Giddings, Franklin H. 1929. *The Mighty Medicine: Superstition and Its Antidote: A New Liberal Education*. New York: Macmillan.

Gillin, John L. 1927. "The Development of Sociology in the United States." *Publications of the American Sociological Society* 21:1-25.

Goldman, Lawrence. 1987. "A Peculiarity of the English? The Social Science Association and the Absence of Sociology in Nineteenth-Century Britain." *Past and Present*, 11:133-171.

Greiger, Roger L. 1986. *To Advance Knowledge*. New York: Oxford University Press.

Gross, Llewellyn, ed. 1959. *Symposium of Sociological Theory*. New York: Harper & Row.

Hare, Peter H. 1985. *A Woman's Quest for Science: Portrait of Anthropologist Elsie Clews Parsons*. New York: Prometheus Books.

Harrison, Shelby H. 1921. "Essentials of a Survey Plan." *Papers and Proceedings of the American Sociological Society* 15:218-220.

Harvey, Lee. 1987. *Myths of the Chicago School of Sociology*. Brookfield, VT: Avebury.

Haskell, Thomas L. 1977. *The Emergence of Professional Social Science: The American Social Science Association and the Nineteenth-Century Crisis of Authority*. Urbana: University of Illinois Press.

Heeren, John William. 1975. "Functional and Critical Sociology: A Study of Two Groups of Contemporary Sociologists." Ph.D. dissertation, Duke University.

Hetrick, Barbara, John Pease, and Richard A. Mathers. 1978. "Historical Notes on the First Regional Sociological Society." *Sociological Forum* 1(Fall):87-93.

Higham, John. 1976. "The Matrix of Specialization." Pp. 1-18 in *The Organization of Knowledge in Modern America 1860-1920*, edited by A. Oleson and J. Voss. Baltimore: Johns Hopkins University Press.

Hinkle, Roscoe. 1980. *Founding Theory of American Sociology, 1881-1915*. Boston: Routledge & Kegan Paul.

Hinkle, Roscoe and Gisella J. Hinkle. 1954. *The Development of Modern Sociology*. New York: Random House.

Hofstadter, Richard and Wilson Smith, eds. 1961. *American Higher Education: A Documentary History*. Chicago: University of Chicago Press.

Horowitz, Irving L. 1963. *Professing Sociology*. Chicago: Aldine.

Horowitz, Irving L. 1974. *The Rise and Fall of Project Camelot; Studies in the Relationship between Social Science and Practical Politics*, rev. ed. Cambridge: MIT Press.

House, Floyd N. 1936. *The Development of Sociology*. Westport, CT: Greenwood Press.

Israels, Belle L. 1912. "Regulation of Public Amusements." *Proceedings of the Academy of Political Science* 2(July):123-126.

Jacoby, Russell. 1987. *The Last Intellectuals: American Culture in the Age of Academe*. New York: Basic Books.

Jencks, Christopher and David Riesman. 1968. *The Academic Revolution*. Garden City, NJ: Doubleday.

Johnson, Guy B. and Guion G. Johnson. 1980. *Research in Service to Society: The First Fifty Years of the Institute for Research in Social Science at the University of North Carolina*. Chapel Hill: University of North Carolina Press.

Jones, Thomas Jesse. 1968. *The Sociology of a New York City Block*. New York: AMS Press. (Reprint edition of 1904, New York, Columbia University Press.)

Kaesler, Dirk. 1985. *Soziologische Abenteuer: Earle Edward Eubank Besucht Europäische Soziologen in Sommer 1934*. Opladen: Westdeutscher Verlag.

Karl, Barry D. 1974. *Charles E. Merriam and the Study of Politics*. Chicago: University of Chicago Press.

Keyssar, Alexander. 1986. *Out of Work: The First Century of Unemployment in Massachusetts*. Cambridge, UK: Cambridge University Press.

Klausner, Samuel Z. 1986. "The Bid to Nationalize American Social Science." Pp. 3-39 in *The Nationalization of the Social Sciences*, edited by Samuel Z. Klausner and Victor M. Lidz. Philadelphia: University of Pennsylvania Press.

Kuhn, Thomas. 1970. *The Structure of Scientific Revolutions*, 2nd ed. Chicago: University of Chicago Press.

Lantz, Herman. 1984. "Continuities and Discontinuities in American Sociology." *The Sociological Quarterly* (Autumn):581-595.

Latour, Bruno. 1987. *Science in Action: How to Follow Scientists and Engineers through Society*. Cambridge, MA: Harvard University Press.

Lazarsfeld, Paul F., Bernard Berelson, and Hazel Gaudet. 1944. *The People's Choice: How the Voter Makes Up His Mind in a Presidential Election*. New York: Duell, Sloan, and Pearce.

Lee, Alfred McClung. 1988. "Steps Taken toward Liberating Sociologists." *Critical Sociology* 15:47-59.

Leiby, James. 1960. *Carroll Wright and Labor Reform: The Origin of Labor Statistics*. Cambridge, MA: Harvard University Press.

Levine, Donald N. 1980. "Introduction." Pp. iii-lxix in *Simmel and Parsons: Two Approaches to the Study of Society*. New York: Arno Press.

Levy, Marion J. 1952. *The Structure of Society*. New Haven, CT: Yale University Press.

Lidz, Victor M. 1986. "Parsons and Empirical Sociology." Pp. 141-182 in *The Nationalization of the Social Sciences*, edited by Samuel Z. Klausner and Victor M. Lidz. Philadelphia: University of Pennsylvania Press.

Lindeman, Edward C. 1924. *Social Discovery: An Approach to the Study of Functional Groups*. New York: Republic.

Lipset, Seymour M., Martin A. Trow, and James S. Coleman. 1962. *Union Democracy: The Internal Politics of the International Typographical Union*. Garden City, NY: Doubleday.

Lockwood, David. 1956. "Some Remarks on 'The Social System.' " *The British Journal of Sociology* 7(June):134-146.

Lundberg, George A. 1947. *Can Science Save Us?* New York: Longmans, Green.

Lyman, Stanford M. 1972. *The Black American in Sociological Thought: A Failure of Perspective*. New York: G. P. Putnam's Sons.

Lyman, Stanford M. 1985. "Henry Hughes and the Southern Foundations of American Sociology." Pp. 1-70 in *Selected Writings of Henry Hughes: Antebellum Southerner, Slavocrat, Sociologist*, edited by Stanford M. Lyman. Jackson: University Press of Mississippi.

Lynd, Robert S. [1939] 1967. *Knowledge for What? The Place of Social Science in American Culture*. Princeton: Princeton University Press.

Lynd, Robert S. and Helen M. Lynd. 1929. *Middletown: A Study in American Culture*. New York: Harcourt, Brace.

MacIver, Robert M. 1942. *Social Causation*. Boston: Ginn.

Malinowski, Bronislaw. 1944. *A Scientific Theory of Culture*. Chapel Hill: University of North Carolina Press.

Matthews, Fred H. 1977. *Quest for an American Sociology: Robert E. Park and the Chicago School*. Montreal: McGill-Queen's University Press.

Mayo-Smith, Richmond. 1895. *Science of Statistics*, Part 1. *Statistics and Sociology*. New York: Macmillan.

Mayo-Smith, Richmond. [1895] 1910. *Statistics and Sociology*. New York: Columbia University Press.

McCartney, James L. 1970. "On Being Scientific: Changing Styles of Presentation of Sociological Research." *American Sociologist* 4:47-50.

McNeill, George E., ed. 1887. *The Labor Movement: The Problem of Today*. Boston: A. M. Bridgman.

Mead, George Herbert. 1934. *Mind, Self, and Society*. Chicago: University of Chicago Press.

Meehl, Paul. 1967. "Theory Testing in Psychology and Physics: A Methodological Paradox." *Philosophy of Science* 34:103-115.

Meehl, Paul. 1986. "What Social Scientists Don't Understand." Pp. 315-338 in *Methodology in Social Science: Pluralisms and Subjectivities*, edited by Donald W. Fiske and Richard A. Shweder. Chicago: University of Chicago Press.

Meroney, W. P. 1931. "The Membership and Program of Twenty-five Years of the American Sociological Society." *Publication of the American Sociological Society* 25:55-67.

Merton, Robert K. 1938. "Social Structure and Anomie." *American Sociological Review* 3:672-682.

Merton, Robert K. 1947. "Selected Problems of Field Work in the Planned Community." *American Sociological Review* 12:304-312.

Merton, Robert K. 1948. "Discussion." *American Sociological Review* 13:164-168.

Merton, Robert K. 1961. *Contemporary Social Problems*. New York: Harcourt, Brace, & World.

Merton, Robert K. 1968. *Social Theory and Social Structure*. New York: The Free Press.

Merton, Robert K. and Daniel Lerner. 1951. "Social Scientists and Research Policy." Pp. 282-307 in *The Policy Sciences*, edited by Daniel Lerner and Harold D. Lasswell. Stanford: Stanford University Press.

Mills, C. Wright. 1951. *White Collar: The American Middle Classes*. New York: Oxford University Press.

Mills, C. Wright. 1956. *The Power Elite*. New York: Oxford University Press.

Mills, C. Wright. 1958. *The Causes of World War Three*. New York: Simon & Schuster.

Mills, C. Wright. 1959. *The Sociological Imagination*. New York: Oxford University Press.

Mills, C. Wright. 1960. *Listen, Yankee: The Revolution in Cuba*, 1st ed. New York: McGraw-Hill.

Mills, C. Wright. 1961, c1960. *Castro's Cuba: The Revolution in Cuba*. London: Secker & Warburt.

Mitchell, Lucy Sprague. 1953. *Two Lives: The Story of Wesley Clair Mitchell and Myself*. New York: Simon & Schuster.

Morgan, J. Graham. 1982. "Preparation for the Advent: The Establishment of Sociology as a Discipline in American Universities in the Late Nineteenth Century." *Minerva* 20 (Spring-Summer):25-58.

Morgan, J. Graham. 1983. "Courses and Texts in Sociology." *Journal of the History of Sociology* 5(1):42-65.

Myrdal, Gunnar. 1962. *An American Dilemma: The Negro Problem and Modern Democracy*. New York: Harper & Row.

Nelson, Lowry. 1969. *Rural Sociology: Its Origin and Growth in the United States*. Minneapolis: University of Minnesota Press.

Neyman, Jerzy. 1934. "On the Two Different Aspects of the Representative Method." *Journal of the Royal Statistical Society* 97:558-625.

Oberschall, Anthony. 1972a. "Introduction: The Sociological Study of the History of Social Research," Pp. 1-14 in *The Establishment of Empirical Sociology: Studies in Continuity, Discontinuity, and Institutionalization*, edited by A. Oberschall. New York: Harper & Row.

Oberschall, Anthony. 1972b. "The Institutionalization of American Sociology." Pp. 187-251 in *The Establishment of Empirical Sociology: Studies in Continuity, Discontinuity, and Institutionalization*, edited by A. Oberschall. New York: Harper & Row.

Odum, Howard W. 1927. *Man's Quest for Social Guidance: The Study of Social Problems*. New York: H. Holt.

Odum, Howard W. 1939. *American Social Problems: An Introduction to the Study of the People and Their Dilemmas*. New York: Holt.

Odum, Howard W. 1951. *American Sociology: The Story of Sociology in the United States through 1950*. Westport, CT: Greenwood Press.

Ogburn, William F. 1922. *Social Change*. New York: B. W. Huebsch.

Ogburn, William F. 1930. "The Folkways of a Scientific Sociology." *Proceeding of the American Sociological Society* 49:589-615.

Ogburn, William F. 1934. "Limitations of Statistics." *American Journal of Sociology* 40:12-20.

Ogburn, William F. and Alexander Goldenweiser, eds. 1927. *The Social Sciences and Their Interrelations*. Boston: Houghton Mifflin.

Ogg, Frederic A. 1928. *Research in the Humanistic and Social Sciences: Report of a Survey Conducted for the American Council of Learned Societies*. New York: Century.

O'Neill, John. 1974. *Making Sense Together: An Introduction to Wild Sociology*. New York: Harper & Row.

Packard, Vance. 1957. *The Hidden Persuaders*. New York: D. McKay.

Park, Robert E. and Ernest W. Burgess. 1924. *Introduction to the Science of Sociology*. Chicago: University of Chicago Press.

Parsons, Philip A. 1936. "Sociological Research and Political Objectives." *Sociology and Social Research* 20:365-368.

Parsons, Talcott. 1937. *The Structure of Social Action*. New York: McGraw-Hill.

Parsons, Talcott. 1948. "The Position of Sociological Theory." *American Sociological Review* 13:156-164.

Parsons, Talcott. 1951. *The Social System*. New York: The Free Press.

Parsons, Talcott. 1959. "Some Problems Confronting Sociology as a Profession." *American Sociological Review* 24:547-559.

Parsons, Talcott. 1968. *The Structure of Social Action: A Study in Social Theory with Special Reference to a Group of Recent European Writers*, vol. 1. New York: The Free Press.

Parsons, Talcott. 1978. *Action Theory and the Human Condition*. New York: The Free Press.

Parsons, Talcott. 1986. "Social Science: A Basic National Resource." Pp. 41-112 in *The Nationalization of the Social Sciences*, edited by Samuel Z. Klausner and Victor M. Lidz. Philadelphia: University of Pennsylvania Press.

Parsons, Talcott, Robert F. Bales, and Edward Shils. 1953. *Working Papers in the Theory of Action*. Glencoe, IL: The Free Press.

Parsons, Talcott and Edward A. Shils, eds. 1951. *Toward a General Theory of Action*. New York: Harper & Row.

Parsons, Talcott and Neil J. Smelser. 1956. *Economy and Society*. New York: The Free Press.

Pearson, Karl. 1900. *The Grammar of Science*, 2nd ed. London: A. & C. Black.

Pease, John and Barbara Hetrick. 1977a. "An Historical Sketch of the Relationship between the Regional Sociological Societies and the American Sociological Association, 1934-1977." *ASA Footnotes* (May):9-10.

Pease, John and Barbara Hetrick. 1977b. "Associations for Whom? The Regionals and the American Sociological Association." *The American Sociologist* 12(February):42-47.

Phelan, John. 1920. *Readings in Rural Sociology*. New York: Macmillan.

Porter, Theodore M. 1986. *The Rise in Statistical Thinking. 1820-1900*. Princeton, NJ: Princeton University Press.

President's Committee on Social Trends. 1933. *Recent Social Trends in the United States*, vol. 1. New York: McGraw-Hill.

Randall, Daniel R. 1888. *Cooperation in Maryland and the South*. Johns Hopkins University Studies in Historical and Political Science, edited by Herbert B. Adams, Sixth Series XI-XII. Baltimore: Johns Hopkins University. (Reprint edition, 1973. New York: Johnson.)

Raushenbush, Winifred. 1979. *Robert E. Park: Biography of a Sociologist*. Durham, NC: Duke University Press.

Rhoades, Lawrence J. 1981. *A History of the American Sociological Association 1905-1980*. Washington, DC: American Sociological Association.

Ricci, David M. 1984. *The Tragedy of Political Science: Politics, Scholarship, and Democracy*. New Haven, CT: Yale University Press.

Rice, Stuart A., ed. 1931. *Methods in Social Science: A Case Book*. Chicago: University of Chicago Press.

Riesman, David. 1950. *The Lonely Crowd: A Study of the Changing American Character*. New Haven, CT: Yale University Press.

Riley, Matilda White. 1960. "Membership of the American Sociological Association, 1950-1959." *American Sociological Review* 25:914-926.

Riley, Matilda White. 1981. "How Old Is Age 75?" *The American Sociologist* 16(February):38-40.

Ritzer, G. 1975. *Sociology and Multiple Paradigm Science*. Boston: Allyn and Bacon.

Ross, Dorothy. 1979. "The Development of the Social Sciences." Pp. 107-138 in *The Organization of Knowledge in Modern America, 1860-1920*, edited by A. Oleson and J. Voss. Baltimore: Johns Hopkins University Press.

Sewell, William H. 1988. "The Changing Institutional Structure of Sociology and My Career." Pp. 119-143 in *Sociological Lives*, edited by Matilda W. Riley. Newbury Park, CA: Sage.

Sewell, William and Robert M. Hauser. 1975. *Education, Occupation, and Earnings: Achievement in the Early Career*. New York: Academic Press.

Shanas, Ethel. 1945. "The American Journal of Sociology through Fifty Years." *American Journal of Sociology* 50 (6):522-533.

Shaw, Albert, 1888. *Cooperation in the Northwest*. Johns Hopkins University Studies in Historical and Political Science, edited by Herbert B. Adams, Sixth Series IV-VI. Baltimore: Johns Hopkins University. (Reprint edition, 1973. New York: Johnson.)

Shenton, Herbert. 1927. *The Practical Application of Sociology: A Study of the Scope and Purpose of Applied Sociology*. New York: Columbia University Press.

Shils, Edward. 1979. "The Order of Learning in the United States: The Ascendancy of the University." Pp. 19-47 in *The Organization of Knowledge in Modern America, 1860-1920*, edited by A. Oleson and J. Voss. Baltimore: Johns Hopkins University Press.

Shinn, Charles Howard. 1888. *Cooperation on the Pacific Coast*. Johns Hopkins University Studies in Historical and Political Science, edited by Herbert B. Adams, Sixth Series IX-X. Baltimore: Johns Hopkins University. (Reprint edition, 1973. New York: Johnson.)

Sibley, Elbridge. 1974. *Social Science Research Council: The First Fifty Years*. New York: Social Science Research Council.

Sills, David L. 1987. "Paul Lazarsfeld 1901-1976." *Biographical Memoirs* 56:251-282.

Simpson, Ida Harper. 1988. *Fifty Years of the Southern Sociological Society: Change and Continuity in a Professional Society*. Athens: University of Georgia Press.

Small, Albion. 1916. "Fifty Years of Sociology in the United States." *American Journal of Sociology* May:1-56.

Small, Albion. 1905/1974. *General Sociology*. New York: Arno.

Small, Albion. 1967. *Origins of Sociology*. New York: Russell & Russell.

Small, Albion and George E. Vincent. 1894. *An Introduction to the Study of Society*. New York: American Book.

Social Science Research Council. 1983. "Research Support and Intellectual Advance in the Social Sciences." *Items* 37(2/3):33-49.

Somit, Albert and Joseph Tanenhaus. 1982. *The Development of American Political Science: From Burgess to Behavioralism*. New York: Irvington.

Sorokin, Pitirim A. 1937. *Social and Cultural Dynamics*, 4 vol. New York: American Book.

Southern, David W. 1987. *Gunnar Myrdal and Black-White Relations: The Use and Abuse of An American Dilemma. 1944-1969*. Baton Rouge: Louisiana State University Press.

Spencer, Herbert. [1852] 1888. *Social Statics*. New York: D. Appleton.

Spencer, Herbert. [1864-1867] 1897. *The Principles of Biology*. New York: D. Appleton.

Spencer, Herbert. 1873. *The Study of Sociology*. New York: Appleton.

Spencer, Herbert. [1874-1896] 1989. *The Principles of Sociology*. New York: D. Appleton.

Spencer, Herbert. [1875-1898] 1904. *The Principles of Ethics*. New York: D. Appleton.

Stern, Bernhard J. 1932. "Giddings, Ward, and Small: An Interchange of Letters." *Social Forces* 10:305-318.

Stern, Barnhard J. 1933. "The Letters of Albion W. Small to Lester F. Ward." *Social Forces* 12:163-173.

Stern, Bernhard J. 1937. "The Letters of Albion W. Small to Lester F. Ward: IV." *Social Forces* 15:305-321.

Stern, Bernhard. 1948. "The Ward-Ross Correspondence III, 1904-1905." *American Sociological Review* 13:82-94.

Stern, Bernhard. 1949. "The Ward-Ross Correspondence IV, 1906-1912." *American Sociological Review* 14:88-119.

Stouffer, Samuel A. 1934. "Sociology and Sampling." Pp. 476-488 in *The Fields and Methods of Sociology*, edited by L. L. Bernard. New York: Farrar & Rinehart.

Stouffer, Samuel A. 1950. "Some Observations on Study Design." *American Journal of Sociology* 5:355-361.

Stouffer, Samuel A. et al. 1949. *The American Soldier*. Princeton, NJ: Princeton University Press.

Stouffer, Samuel A. 1963. "Methods of Research Used by American Behavioral Scientists." Pp. 65-76 in *The Behavioral Sciences Today*, edited by Bernard Berelson. New York: Basic Books.

Sumner, William Graham. 1907. *Folkways*. New York: Ginn.

Sumner, William Graham and Albert Galloway Keller. 1927. *The Science of Society*, 4 vol. New Haven, CT: Yale University Press.

Taylor, Carl C. 1919. *The Social Survey: Its History and Methods*. Social Science Series 3. *University of Missouri Bulletin* 20 (October).

Thomas, W. I. and Florian Znaniecki. 1918. *The Polish Peasant in Europe and America*, 5 vol. Chicago: University of Chicago Press.

Turner, Jonathan H. 1979. "Toward a Social Physics." *Humbolt Journal of Social Relations* 7(Fall/Winter):123-139.

Turner, Jonathan H. 1981. "Returning to 'Social Physics': Illustrations for the Work of George Herbert Mead." *Current Perspectives in Social Theory* 2:153-186.

Turner, Jonathan H. 1984. *Societal Stratification: A Theoretical Analysis*. New York: Columbia University Press.

Turner, Jonathan H. 1985. "In Defense of Positivism." *Sociological Theory* 3(Fall):24-30.

Turner, Jonathan H. 1986. *The Structure of Sociological Theory*, 4th ed. Chicago: Dorsey Press.

Turner, Jonathan H. 1988. "The Mixed Legacy of the Chicago School of Sociology." *Sociological Perspectives* 31(3):325-338.

Turner, Jonathan H. and Alexandra Maryanski. 1979. *Functionalism*. Menlo Park, CA: Benjamin Cummings.

Turner, Jonathan H. and Alexandra Maryanski. 1988. "Is Neofunctionalism Really Functional?" *Sociological Theory* 6(1):110-121.

Turner, Jonathan H. and Stephen Park Turner. In press. *American Sociology: Its History, Structure, and Substance*. Warsaw: Polish Scientific Publishers.

Turner, Stephen. 1990a. "The Strange Life and Hard Times of the Concept of General Theory in Sociology: A Short History of Hope." In *General Theory and Its Critics*, edited by Steven Seidman and David Wagner. London: Basil Blackwell.

Turner, Stephen. 1990b. "The World of the Academic Quantifiers: The Columbia University Family and Its Connections." In *The Social Survey in Historical Perspective: Britain and the United States 1880-1940*, edited by Kevin Boles, Kathryn Skiar, and Martin Bulmer. Cambridge: Cambridge University Press.

Turner, Stephen. 1990c. "Forms of Patronage." In *Theories of Science in Society*, edited by Susan Cozzens and Thomas F. Gieryn. Bloomington: Indiana University Press.

Vidich, Arthur J. and Stanford M. Lyman. 1985, *American Sociology: Worldly Rejections of Religion and Their Directions*. New Haven, CT: Yale University Press.

Ward, Lester. 1883. *Dynamic Sociology*. New York: D. Appleton.

Warner, Amos G. 1888. *Three Phases of Cooperation in the West*. Johns Hopkins University Studies in Historical and Political Science, edited by Herbert B. Adams, Sixth Series VII-VIII. Baltimore: Johns Hopkins University. (Reprint edition, 1973. New York: Johnson.)

Weber, Max. 1968. *Economy and Society*. New York: Bedminister.

Weed, Frank J. 1979. "Bureaucratization as Reform: The Case of the Public Welfare Movement, 1900-1929." *The Social Science Journal* 16(October):79-89.

Wells, Richard H. and Steven J. Picou. 1981. *American Sociology: Theoretical and Methodological Structure*. Washington, DC: University Press of America.

Wespsiec, Jan. 1983. *Sociology: An International Bibliography of Serial Publications 1880-1980*. London: Mansell.

White, Leonard Dupee, ed. 1930. *The New Social Science*. Chicago: University of Chicago Press.

Whitley, Richard. 1984. *The Intellectual and Social Organization of the Sciences*. Oxford: Clarendon Press.

Wiley, Norbert. 1986. "Early American Sociology and the Polish Peasant." *Sociological Theory* 4(1):20-40.

Willcox, Walter F. 1891. *The Divorce Problem: A Study in Statistics*. Studies in History, Economics and Public Law, Vol. 1. New York: Columbia University Press. (AMS Reprint, 1969).

Winch, Peter. 1958. *The Idea of a Social Science and Its Relation to Philosophy*. London: Routledge & Kegan Paul.

Wirth, Lewis. 1938. "Urbanism as a Way of Life." *American Journal of Sociology* 1:46-63.

Woldring, Henk E. S. 1987. *Karl Mannheim, the Development of His Thought: Philosophy, Sociology, and Social Ethics*. New York: St. Martin's.

Wright, Carroll D. 1909. *Outline of Practical Sociology*, 7th ed., rev. New York: Longman's, Green.

Wright, Robert Joseph. 1974. *Principia, or, Basis of Social Science*. New York: Arno Press.

Young, Donald. 1948. "Limiting Factors in the Development of the Social Sciences." *Proceedings of the American Philosophical Society* 92:325-335.

Yule, G. Udny. 1899. "On the Correlation of Total Pauperism with 'Proportion of Out-Relief.' " *The Economic Journal* 5:603-611.

Zetterberg, Hans L. 1956. *Sociology in the United States of America: A Trend Report*. Paris: UNESCO.

ARCHIVAL REFERENCES

Bernard, L. L. *Papers*. University of Chicago, Chicago. (Cited as BPUC.)

Duke University Archives. Duke University Library, Durham, NC.

Keppel, Frederick. *Reminiscences*. Oral History Collection, Columbia University, New York.

Lazarsfeld, Paul F. *Tapes*. William E. Weiner Oral History Library of the American Jewish Committee, New York. (Cited as PFLW.)

Lynd, Helen M. *Tapes*. Oral History Collection, Columbia University, New York. (Cited as HML.)

MacIver, Robert M. *Tapes*. Oral History Collection, Columbia University, New York. (Cited as RMI.)

Stouffer, Samuel A. *Papers*. Archives, Harvard University, Cambridge, MA. (Cited as SAS.)

Index

Abel, Theodore, 130
Abolitionists, 13-14, 16
Action, concept of, 72, 74, 84, 111, 122, 132
Adler, Mortimer, 76
Adorno, Theodor W., 100
Agriculture, Department of, see United States
Agricultural Research Stations, 91-2, 104
Albury, R., 120
Allport, Floyd, 106
American Dilemma, The, 69, 94, 97-100
American Anthropological Association, 80
American Association of University Professors, 44
American Catholic Sociological Society, 61
American Council of Learned Societies, 148
American Economic Association, 28, 54-55
American Historical Association, 28, 80
American Jewish Committee, 100
American Journal of Sociology (AJS), 29, 60, 67, 80-1, 149-50, 159
American Political Science Association (APSA), 28, 53, 55, 58, 81
American Psychological Association, 80
American Sociological Review (ASR), 60, 149, 152, 159

American Sociological Society(ASS)/Association(ASA), 13, 16, 40, 54, 58-60, 64, 75, 81-2, 127, 145, 148-160, 168, 171, 177-8; committees of, 53-4, 149, 156; constitution of, 149-50; democratization of, 157; founding of, 28; leadership, 30; organization of, 139, 148, 151-56; membership, 29, 58-61, 86, 88, 129, 138-40, 148-52, 154, 177-8; sections, 148-50, 153, 158; staff, 150
American Statistical Association, 28-9, 80; Journal of, 80
American Studies Programs, 195
Amusements, public, 78
Anomie, 131, 175, 189
Applied sociology, 149, 179; see also Policy, Evaluation research
Archeology, 36
Attitude, 21, 69, 74-7, 105-6, 175
Audience, 16, 24, 31, 41, 58, 64, 79, 81, 109, 122, 126-8, 136-7, 182-3, 195
Authoritarian Personality, The, 100

Bain, Read, 73, 125
Bachelor's degree, see Student demand
Baker, Newton, 98
Bannister, Robert, 19, 36, 60, 66, 103
Barnard College, 80
Barnes, Harry Elmer, 62-3, 71, 78, 84, 103, 122, 190

213

About the Authors

Jonathan H. Turner is Professor of Sociology at the University of California at Riverside. He received his B.S. degree in sociology from the University of California at Santa Barbara in 1965, his M.A. from Cornell University in 1966, and his Ph.D. in 1968. He has been at the University of California at Riverside since 1969.

He is author of some 16 books, editor of several more, and contributor to numerous articles in journals and chapters in collections. Most of his research revolves around the development and analysis of sociological theory, although he has substantive interests in ethnic stratification, social stratification in general, societal evolution, and American social structure. The present book represents his effort to understand why sociology has increasingly become hostile to scientific theory, or to the prospects of being a true science.

Stephen Park Turner is Graduate Research Professor in the Department of Philosophy at the University of South Florida, Tampa. He has held appointments in sociology departments at the University of Notre Dame and Boston University as well as the University of South Florida, and in Science and Technology studies at Virginia Tech. He has published extensively on Weber, Durkheim, and the philosophy of social science. His most recent book is *The Search for a Methodology of Social Science: Durkheim, Weber, and the Nineteenth Century Problem of Cause, Probability, and Action*, published in the series *Boston Studies in the Philosophy of Science* in 1986.